The First Bearmas

by dhtreichler

Granma and the Attic Bear

Today, Sarajane "SJ" Wilcox celebrates her seventh birthday. Now Granma needs a special pan to make a little cake. "A small cake. No leftovers," Granma tells SJ with her slightly French enunciation. They make their way up the narrow and steep attic stairs of the meandering old house. SJ doesn't understand why her grandmother hates leftovers. She and her mother never have them. Even though she seldom goes to bed hungry, rarely does she go to bed not wishing there had been more. Granma opens the door into the dark loft. She coughs as the dirt and dust greet them like old friends.

"I like leftovers ... usually," SJ responds to her grandmother. Granma seems old to SJ, much older than her mother. But for some reason she doesn't have white hair like all the grandmothers on TV and in the books she reads. This is one of the mysteries she wants to solve.

Granma and Mama have been talking about her new school a lot, as she and her mother just moved. Granma seems to think being in a class with different children should be just great. "A chance to make new friends", she says. On the other hand, Mama doesn't seem as happy about her being "with rich kids," as Granma keeps describing them. When they talk about it, SJ hears the tension between these two most important women in her life. She doesn't know who is right. SJ thinks this school is not much different than the last one. The kids talk and play with her. But then it's only been a few weeks.

"Now, where did I pack that cake pan?" Granma takes a quick look around, spots a box in a corner and heads off to it. The attic is Granma's secret place. She never comes here except to find something she rarely uses, or to pack away something she seldom intends to use

3

again. SJ remembers her saying, as she climbs the stairs carrying whatever is about to be hidden away, "But you just never know…" SJ's eyes adjust to the darkness. She scans for an old chest she found last time. Granma wouldn't let her open it. She remembers boxes were piled on top.

SJ hears Granma rustling though boxes, humming "Happy Birthday." SJ spots her objective, which remains in the same spot. She expects the boxes on top to be heavy but lifts them easily. SJ places them one by one on the floor. She struggles to lift the heavy lid to the worn old wooden chest. As the lid comes open, she is surprised to find a treasure trove of old clothes. SJ pulls out a few items, examining each as she holds it up. The clothes appear to fit a girl only a little older than herself. But with a frown SJ studies the patterns in the fabric and notes the buttons and zippers missing from her own simple garments.

"I could wear these, Granma," SJ proudly calls out.

"No, dear. Put them back. They're not for you to play with." The response seems a bit harsh, but Granma gets that way sometimes. SJ starts to put them away, when she notices a hairy right ear tucked in under everything. It belongs to a small dusty brown bear with button eyes and white thread stitching.

SJ drops the clothes and digs out the welcoming bear. She hugs him tightly then holds him out to look at him. "Hello, mister bear. I bet you've been looking all over for a little girl of your own."

Movement catches SJ's eye as her grandmother seems to turn with surprise. SJ looks longer and realizes she has never seen the sad expression that haunts the older woman's eyes. SJ considers this for a brief moment, but doesn't remark upon it. The bear dancing before her retains much more interest than an unusual look.

Suddenly Granma appears behind her, seizes the bear in mid frolic, drops it into the chest, closes the lid and situates herself upon the closed chest. The sudden appearance of her grandmother startles SJ, who takes a moment to realize her new found friend has disappeared.

"Granma! We're having fun."

"That's not your bear," comes the firm response SJ knows is intended to end the discussion. However, SJ seldom obeys when she doesn't understand or agree.

"But he's lonely. He wants someone to play with." Her almost indignant response pours out.

Granma gets up and takes her hand to lead her away from the chest. "He had his someone, once." The distant explanation doesn't satisfy SJ, who pulls her hand away and steps back toward the chest.

"Why can't I play with him?" SJ starts to open the lid again in search of the bear, when Granma takes her hand more firmly and literally drags her screaming away. "Ow!" precedes the ka-chunk of the falling lid. "You're hurting me, Granma,"

Granma loosens the grip just a bit. SJ bolts away. But this time Granma swoops the girl off her feet and carries her back to the large boxes of pots and pans.

"Granma, let me go! That bear's calling me. Can't you hear him? He's so lonely in that chest."

"He's fine. Now help me find the little cake pan we use for your birthday cake. You know which one I'm talking about."

"Granma! The bear!" SJ wrestles to free herself of Granma's grasp, but the older woman takes SJ's chin and turns her face to get her attention.

"Either you forget the bear and help me find the pan, or you'll have no birthday cake. What's it going to be?"

SJ doesn't hesitate with her response "I want the bear…"

Assumptions

An exhausted Genevieve looks much older than her twenty-four years. Deep circles highlight her hazel eyes and long golden hair. Always thin, she borders on too thin. When overtired she must keep moving or fall asleep where ever she finds herself. Maybe her nervous habit of twisting strands of hair is enough. Of late she has found even that doesn't keep her focused when driving to her mother's house like tonight. She turns the volume up on the radio, but no change in the volume results. Her rusty and beat-up twelve-year-old Honda Civic may finally be on its last legs. Genevieve dreads having to get another car. *A car should be like a microwave, just plug it in and it goes forever.* But she knows that isn't the case. She has to figure out how to get the money to replace it or she will soon be taking the bus … again.

She pulls the car into the driveway of a familiar old house. She remembers it was built around nineteen hundred by a doctor, whose name eludes her. This old house embodies the memories of the best and worst moments of her life. *Maybe that house really does represent who I am.* After parking the car, she gets out. She looks up at the widow's walk, taking it in for a long moment. *I'm not a widow. Not really.* She shakes her head and walks up the steps. Crossing the rickety porch, she uses her key to open the door.

"Mom, SJ. I'm here," she calls, not hearing the usual commotion from her daughter, which makes her curious. As she turns into the kitchen, she finds SJ sitting at the table, He daughter displays a frown and crossed arms. Her mother stands at the sink preparing dinner with her back to her granddaughter. *I've seen this movie too.*

Genevieve smiles anyway. "Happy Birthday, kiddo." She goes to

6

her daughter, kisses her on the cheek, followed by a big hug. "I love you."

SJ points to her grandmother. "She won't let me have the bear."

Genevieve moves closer to her mother, to whom she gives a kiss on the cheek, then asks, "What's all this about a bear?"

Granma continues making dinner. "It's almost ready. Better get washed up."

Genevieve leads her daughter to the front hall bathroom. SJ doesn't need to, but out of habit steps up on the step stool Genevieve's father made for his daughter and her sister when they were small. SJ leans over the sink, washes her hands with soap, then turns, holding them out for her mother to dry.

"You and Granma having a fight?" Genevieve asks neutrally.

"The attic bear wants to come out and play." SJ appears frustrated. She's more than a little angry that Granma won't give her what she wants.

"Oh, that bear." Genevieve nods her head in sudden understanding. She reaches over SJ, washes her own hands, and then dries them. "That bear's a problem."

"Why? Is he a bad bear?" SJ demands to know.

Genevieve hugs her. "No, from what I remember he actually was a very good bear. He always minded his manners, was polite and a good conversationalist."

"Was he your bear?" SJ becomes cautiously excited and hopeful.

"No. I never had a bear." Genevieve responds neutrally but with a hint of disappointment.

SJ hugs her mother. "I'm sorry. Maybe you would have been

7

happier if he were your bear."

Genevieve kisses SJ. "I'm happy. I have you. And you're much more fun than a silly old bear." Genevieve tickles her daughter, who laughs and pushes her hand away.

SJ will not abandon the subject. "Didn't you want a bear?"

Genevieve thinks back. "You know when I was your age Granma was very busy. I spent most of my time reading books. I always had new friends in all the stories I read."

"I like to read," SJ offers.

"I know you do. It makes me happy to see how much you read." Another hug, only this time, SJ throws her arms around her mother's neck and hugs back.

As they walk out of the bathroom, Genevieve asks her daughter, "So what did Granma give you for your birthday?"

"A spanking."

A surprised Genevieve asks, "And why did she give you that?"

"Because I didn't listen to her." While the response is defiant, Genevieve hears the regret as well as SJ's expectation of a coming reprimand from her mother.

"So, did you say you're sorry and won't do that again?" Genevieve tries to make it soft.

"No," she says simply.

Knowing where this is going, Genevieve loudly exhales before responding. "Well, I think you need to do that right now."

Genevieve sees SJ prepared for this. The birthday girl looks up at her mother ready to appeal, but Genevieve shakes her head to let her know none will be granted. SJ reluctantly and contritely goes over to where her Granma puts the last of the meal on the table.

"I'm sorry, Granma. I won't disobey you again." Granma kneels down next to her granddaughter and gives her a hug.

"That's all I want to hear." Granma gives SJ a quick kiss on the cheek. "Okay, everything's ready." The older woman gestures to the table for everyone to sit.

"Everything smells good, Mom," Genevieve remarks as she sits down and puts a napkin across the lap of her daughter first, and then herself.

"No leftovers, so I expect you two to eat everything." Granma replaced the traditional blessing a long time ago. As Genevieve remembers, it happened shortly after her father left. In fact, their last fight was over a blessing on Thanksgiving. After asking the Lord's blessing for all the usual things, Genevieve's mother asked the Lord to bless Doris Gedding with a conscience. Genevieve had never seen her father get so angry. His face turned crimson and he exploded from his chair. He threw the napkin at his wife and storming out without so much as a good-bye. Genevieve remembers not understanding what had happened until much later. She learned her father was living with Doris Gedding and had filed for a divorce.

Genevieve and her mother talk in the comfortable den. SJ reads a book out loud to herself at the kitchen table. The open door permits them to hear SJ, but they can't see her. No fire fills the fireplace, so the usually warm room has a chilling effect on Genevieve.

"I think you need to find someone else to care for her while you're at work," her mother, in her typical fashion just lays it right out there.

"Mom, I can't do that. I don't make enough to cover the bills I have, let alone add another payment," just spills out of Genevieve.

"You made the bed you sleep in."

The all too familiar response from her mother grates on Genevieve. She wants to lash back but she needs her mother to help her with SJ. She can't let her temper get away from her. So she counts to three before responding. "I know, Mom. I'm up for a promotion. If I get it, maybe I can find someone for a day or two a week. But think of SJ. She needs stability in her caregiver."

Her mother's eyes assume a hooded look that Genevieve has seen all too often before. Genevieve knows the dance between them will continue with both knowing what the other wants, but neither willing to give it. Of course one or the other will bend just before the relationship breaks.

"A promotion? Frankly I'm surprised they'd consider you."

Genevieve hears her mother's challenge to her hopes. Having been disappointed so many times before, she knows her mother wants to prepare her for another possible disappointment. "I work longer and harder than anyone else. They can't afford to see me leave and go to a competitor." Genevieve gives the rationalization for her mother to consider.

"I wouldn't have such a high opinion of myself, if I were you."

Genevieve listens to the things her mother says between the words. A new undertone she hasn't heard before, surfaces. It's almost as if her mother doesn't want her to succeed on her terms. As if the stranger before her wants to punish her for something she did. Have an illegitimate child maybe? Will her mother ever forgive her? Will Genevieve ever forgive herself?

"What is it, mother? What are you trying to tell me?" Genevieve decides not to continue guessing.

Her mother's hooded eyes don't move in response to the question. A long silence sits between them until her mother formulates a response. "I want you to be responsible for yourself and your daughter. I need a life of my own."

Genevieve always assumed her mother would stand with her until she established herself. The realization the day may have come and she could be completely on her own, deflates her. She struggles for a response. Nothing comes to her that she doesn't instantly censor. Her head perks up upon hearing SJ reading, then suddenly laughing at something.

"Contrary to your approach, I might remarry if I can find the right man" Her mother continues. "Or I might take a different job where I have to go in to work. But I can't do either when I'm watching SJ five and six days a week while you work."

The words land upon Genevieve as if from an alien that hasn't yet learned to communicate with earthlings. At first, the words don't make sense to her. Then, the meaning suddenly crashes through, tilting the world in a different direction. Now nothing seems safe. The predictable and barely manageable life she so carefully, and with great difficulty constructed, disappears before her eyes.

Genevieve needs time to consider her mother's request. She calls to her daughter, "SJ. Can you find your things? We need to get home and to bed."

SJ calls back to her mother, "But I haven't had my birthday cake."

Genevieve's mother answers that one, "You chose not to have me make you one, remember? Up in the attic? You'll just have to wait until next year."

Genevieve can't believe what she hears, "Mom? No birthday cake?"

The hooded eyes open wider. Her mother looks at Genevieve but doesn't offer an answer.

11

The Milk's Gone

SJ finishes reading the story to herself as Genevieve drives the rusting Honda through the dark old tree-lined neighborhoods. When finished, SJ closes the book then looks up at her mother. She can see her mother's eyes are red. Her mother hasn't said a word since they got into the car. Never a good sign. SJ hesitates before asking.

"Momma?"

"What, SJ?"

The girl detects a frightened response from her mother, but decides to ask the question that preoccupies her. "Why won't Granma let me have that bear?" She watches her mother's reaction. She quickly resigns herself to not getting an answer. But reacts with surprise when one finally arrives.

"I told you that was a special bear. You can't expect Granma to give you things that are special to her."

"But today's my birthday. I'm a special person on my birthday. You told me that."

Genevieve smiles through her watery eyes at her daughter. "Yes, you're very special. And not just on your birthday."

SJ listens, tries to find an opening to get the bear. "But if I'm a special person and this is a special day, don't two specials mean I should get what I want?"

Genevieve shakes her head. "It doesn't work that way, Sarajane."

"You never call me Sarajane except when you're mad. What did I do?"

Genevieve turns a corner before answering, but SJ notices her mother catches a quick glimpse of her before doing so. "Do I sound mad at you?"

SJ studies her mother for a moment. "No, and that's confusing me."

"I'm not mad at you. Today just hasn't been a good day for me. I'm sorry if I'm taking it out on you." Genevieve seems genuinely regretful.

"It's my birthday, so why wasn't it a good day for you?" SJ watches her mother pause before responding.

"I guess I assumed some things I shouldn't have. You know how some things just always seem to be there, like the apartment and this car? So you expect they will be there the next day, and the next."

SJ can't look at her mother. She stares out the window for a long time, thinking about what her mother said. Then she asks, "Are we moving, again?"

Genevieve shakes her head and finally a small smile appears. "No, dear. We aren't moving. I'm sorry, the problems adults have are sometimes hard to explain. Even I don't understand them most of the time."

"But things are bad, aren't they?"

"Things are great with us. Today's your birthday. We've gotten through seven years together. Hopefully we'll have another dozen or so before you find the man of your dreams. Then you'll live happily ever after."

SJ puzzles on her mother's comment, "But why didn't my daddy take you away with him so you could live happily ever after?" SJ watches as a tear streams down her mother's cheek.

Genevieve suddenly pulls herself together, "You'll find the man of your dreams. He will take you away to live happily ever after."

SJ considers her mother's response, but still has a question, "What if I don't want to go away. Can't I stay here with you? Just like you stayed with Granma?"

"You can stay with me as long as you want, kiddo. But a day will come when you'll meet someone wonderful and you'll want to be with him."

SJ looks out the windshield at the dark street, "Okay."

A frail smile appears on Genevieve's face that makes SJ glad she was able to make her mother happy, if only for a moment.

The tiny studio apartment seems barely large enough for one. Really just two rooms with areas for their beds. No walls separate the living areas. A single plant grows in the flowerbox outside the kitchen window. It contributes the only real color seen in the drab and bare room.

Neatly folded clothes sit in piles at the end of SJ's mattress on the floor. Across the room her mother's clothes hang from a makeshift rod at the head of her mattress. SJ loves to look at the clothes her mother wears. She dreams of wearing them. Many her mother wore in high school and were hand-me-downs. There was never enough money. And that situation remains for them.

SJ has her pajamas on. She goes to the refrigerator for a glass of milk. "Mom!" she calls without looking around, "The milk's gone."

Her mother pokes her head out of the bathroom door, "Sorry, I didn't get a chance to stop at the store on the way to Granma's."

SJ slams the door, which she knows will evoke a comment from her mother. "I want some milk."

"SJ, I can't make it magically appear. You'll have to wait until tomorrow. Remind me when I pick you up from Granma's," comes across less angrily than SJ expects. She crosses over to the bathroom and enters, leaning against her mother. She watches Mama inspect her own face in the mirror.

"Why do you do that?" SJ asks to get her mother to talk to her.

"What sweetie?" Genevieve asks absently.

"Look at yourself like that. Don't you know what you look like?" SJ puts her arm around her mother, to increase the contact and make sure she can't ignore her. The hoped for response comes as her mother kneels down to talk to her, "I want to make sure I look as good as I can."

"Why?" SJ just wants to keep the attention.

"No one wants to see me with my hair all messed up...." her mother musses her hair to illustrate her point, "...or big blemishes on my face, or my eyebrows growing together or hair growing out of my ears and nose."

SJ laughs as her mother tickles her, then gives her a hug. "But you need to get to bed now." Her mother turns her around and gives her a playful swat on her behind. But SJ craves attention. She turns back to her mother and asks, "Why does that bear make Granma sad?"

Her mother's voice sounds weary. "As we get older we remember things more."

SJ doesn't understand, only knows that her mother didn't give her the answer she was looking for. "So why does that bear make Granma sad?"

Her mother dances around it one more time, "Granma doesn't want to remember things that make her sad."

SJ won't let go. "Why that bear, Momma?"

Genevieve rises to end the conversation, "Maybe when you're older we can talk about the bear and why Granma is sad about it."

"I am older. Today's my birthday and I'm seven." SJ watches the smile come back to her mother, who nods and responds, "Yes, happy birthday. You're seven and I'm tired and we both need to get some sleep. So it's off to bed with you." Her mother herds her out of the bathroom, chases her across the room to her bed. SJ jumps on the mattress and sits down. Her mother pulls up the covers. SJ snuggles down. Her mother kisses her good night. "Sleep tight, kiddo. Another busy day tomorrow."

SJ tries one more delay tactic. "Is your day going to be busy?" But her mother doesn't want to let the conversation continue.

"Every day is busy at work. That's why I'm late picking you up so often. No rest for the wicked," her mother concludes.

"But you're not wicked," SJ protests.

A weary agreement confuses SJ. "I hope not anymore." Her mother kisses her good night again. SJ watches her mother pick up the book beside her mattress. She does that every night, read for a while, although most nights SJ falls asleep before her mother finishes reading. And tonight is no exception.

Arrival of the Cheerleader

Acres of open cubicles interspersed with large plants under the skylights and fluorescent lights form the Richland Insurance Company offices. Supposedly this approach gives it a naturalistic feel while maintaining cost efficient density. Nearly all of the mostly women who work here, including Genevieve, refer to it as the jungle -- for more than one reason.

Genevieve sits in the middle of the fourth floor, the claims division. This group gathers the information about a claim, investigates it, and confirms the information. Afterwards, an adjuster assigns a value to the claim and pays it. Normally, Genevieve does the first three parts of the job, but not the last one. She must be an adjuster to assign a value to the claim. To be an adjuster she needs to have a college degree, although a few of the older women don't have one either.

Genevieve joined Richland as a mail clerk shortly after SJ was born. That was the only job she qualified for other than cleaner at the time. But she immediately befriended Dean Parrish, the bearish-built office supervisor. He instantly recognized her curious mind and disarming charm as an effective set of skills for an adjuster. Within a month he promoted her to an investigator trainee. Nearly seven years later she consistently gets among the highest ratings from Dean. She knows Dean likes her. He probably thinks of her as a daughter. Although a few times he made comments that would indicate possibly a different regard for her that she doesn't care to explore.

Four months earlier, Sandy Lewis, the adjuster with whom Genevieve worked the last two years, left for a maternity leave. Even though she doesn't have the necessary degree, Dean let Genevieve fill in for Sandy. He justified the move to management by indicating he would watch Genevieve carefully and monitor more of her calls than usual. After the first week he started monitoring less of her calls than the others, a source of pride and recognition for Genevieve. But then Dean told her a week ago that Sandy decided to stay home with her little boy. Now he has the opportunity to fill her job. To Genevieve this is the big test – whether Dean will appoint her to the adjuster role. If he were the only one making the decision, she believes he would give it to her. But she knows others must be convinced, as it would be an exception to policy. She knows all too well management hates to make exceptions. It gives hope to those who should have none. That includes her without a high school diploma or degree, even though she does the work as well or better than anyone else.

She knows the person Dean needs to convince is the Vice President of Claims, Andrea Stuart. Pretty much whatever Andrea wants, Andrea gets. But Andrea has her favorites. Dean is not one of them. Genevieve tried, but has never been able to establish a relationship with Andrea. She thinks Andrea only wants to deal with her direct reports. Although from time-to-time Genevieve sees her in one of the adjuster's cubicles chatting up a storm about one thing or another. This, Andrea has never done with Sandy or herself.

Just then Genevieve sees Dean's thinning brown hair over the tops of the cubicles. She notes his usual heavy footstep sounds more deliberate as he approaches Genevieve's day-time home. His friendly smile seems missing as he pokes his head into her area. Dread fills her. She holds up her index finger and turns away to finish her call. "That's right Misses Sanchez; you should receive your check within the week for the full amount we discussed, one thousand, two hundred and twelve dollars. . . . That's correct. It's been my pleasure working with you to settle this claim. We appreciate your business. Thank you, Misses Sanchez."

Genevieve quickly types the settlement and closure note into the computer case file before she turns to look at Dean, bracing for what she fears.

Dean seems to take in her expression and body language. He closes his eyes for a moment, then nods for her to follow him.

She does so. As they walk back towards his office she asks, "How's your day going so far?"

"Just another sunny day in paradise." She listens carefully to the tone of his response, which she takes as code for not the way he wanted it to go. Hearing that, she decides to complete the rest of the short journey in silence.

Once in his office, Dean motions for her to close the door and take a seat. They have done this hundreds of times before. Usually, they discuss her progress or a specific claim. Sometimes they just chat about an upcoming weekend or something in the news. But not this time. She heard from Beth, one of the other intake specialists, that Dean concluded the interviews for Sandy's spot. The recommendation went up to Andrea on Friday. She hopes against hope this is not the subject today, but suspects otherwise, based on his demeanor.

She apprehensively studies Dean as he looks at a closed file on his desk. He remains silent, apparently gathering his thoughts. She decides to ask a question first. "Have you seen this month's stats yet?"

He nods but still doesn't look up at her. "You have the shortest resolution time, lowest settlement of initial claims values and highest post closure customer satisfaction, as you have since Sandy went on leave. Congratulations."

"But…" she wants to force the undertone out and get it over with.

"Andrea selected an outside hire, Janie Peterson." This comes across with a clear indication he didn't recommend it.

Genevieve's eyes tear up. She blinks away the tears as she regains her composure. "She have a lot of experience?"

Dean shakes his head, "New grad. This will be her first job."

Genevieve rockets out of her chair and leans across his desk, "She took someone with no experience over me with nearly seven years?"

Dean looks sad, offers advice, "You know the company policy. Maybe this is the wake-up call. At least, get the high school diploma. Then start on the degree."

Genevieve stands back up, but doesn't sit down, "Haven't I shown you I can do the job without it?"

"You're the best in my department," he confirms.

"The best in the company, according to those statistics," she points out, now more hurt than angry. Dean nods, but won't look at her. She spins around and opens the door.

"Where are you going?" He wants to know.

"Back to my desk. I suppose to add insult to injury I'll have to train this new grad?" She stares at him almost daring him to confirm it.

"I suspect if you give her a chance, you could become good friends." Dean remarks as he picks up the file and puts it into the out-basket on his desk.

"And if I want a recommendation?" She throws in to let him know what she thinks about the situation.

"You'll get the highest recommendation I've ever given anyone . . . whenever you finally ask for it." He responds, challenging her right back.

Genevieve hears what he's saying. A recommendation will only go so far without the education. She settles back down. "So when does she start?"

Dean looks at his watch. "I suspect she came in while we've been talking. If she didn't, she's late."

Genevieve steps through the door. Slams it shut behind her. As she walks back to her cubicle, she notices people in their cubicles peering out to see who slammed Dean's door. She knows the word will be all over within minutes that she didn't get the promotion. But she can also guess most will be happy she didn't, since she will no longer count against their statistics.

When she reaches her cubicle, Genevieve hears voices in Sandy's cube. She decides to take a peek at what a Janie Peterson might look like. *Not that I'm really curious or anything.* She walks next door to Sandy's old cubicle. Sure enough, Allison, the pleasant blonde from HR, sits across from – *oh, no – not a cheerleader type* -- brunette with a big smile, perfect body and face. *This is not going to work.* Genevieve remembers Andrea was president of her college sorority. The rumors were that the owner's wife had been president of that same sorority. She should have expected this.

Allison notices Genevieve's approach to the cubical. "Oh, and Janie, this is Genevieve Wilcox. She'll do the intake and investigations for you." Janie turns and gives Genevieve the once-over, maintaining the smile, but not giving any indication of what she really thinks. *This is going to be just like High School all over again, isn't it you bitch?* Genevieve thinks, but realizes she can't show any hostility – at least not yet. "Hi. Welcome to the RIC."

Janie doesn't follow the greeting, "The what?"

"Richland Insurance Company, the RIC."

Allison wants to complete the introductions, "Janie comes to us from the University of Texas in Austin."

Genevieve reaches out to shake hands. "Good school, from what I hear."

Janie responds to the offered hand and replies, "Big school and all that."

Genevieve nods in confirmation of her previous thoughts. "Well Dean wants me to work out a training plan with you. So when you get settled in why don't you come on over. I've got some things to clean up this morning but should have time this afternoon."

Janie's smile fades for only a moment. It returns as she sits down to complete her conversation with Allison. "That sounds great. Get right to it."

I've got to find another job. A disappointed Genevieve tries ineffectively to hide her feelings as she returns to her own cubicle. To the list of claims to process today.

As she sits down at her computer the phone rings. "Richland Insurance, Genevieve Wilcox. How may I help you today?" It turns out to be one of her more troublesome clients. The older man seems convinced that the insurance company wants to keep him from getting what's coming to him. She worked hard to win over his confidence. The post claim survey will barbeque her if she can't find some way of making him believe she really has done everything possible for him. But with the turn of events, *what difference does it make?*

She considers turning him over to Janie right now. *Let it be a trial by fire.* But the image of Janice Ramsey, who taught her the ropes, comes to mind. She knows she has the responsibility to do the same for Janie. *It's not her fault. She has a degree and I don't.* That realization doesn't make it any easier to accept.

The troublesome customer interrupts her thoughts. "What's the problem with my claim? You people don't seem to think getting my money to me is a priority. I could have the car fixed by now if you weren't dragging your feet or whatever it is that you people drag up there."

Genevieve remembers Janice saying to her to always start every conversation with a customer by putting on a smile. Keep that smile until after the conversation is over. And then to thank the customer by name. So she puts on her smile and says, "No, sir, no problems. Now what I have been able to determine is if we simply replace two additional parts, we can complete the work quicker and the total cost will be less. That's good for you and for us. You'll have your car back sooner and it will last longer.

Genevieve feels better getting back to work. *The work will make it better.* But then she realizes she was counting on the extra money to replace her car. Give her mother a few days off. *That's not going to happen now. But I can't think about that. Have to complete this claim. Get this man's car back to him.*

She rejoins the conversation on the phone. "Yes, we use remanufactured parts, but they will have a longer life than the parts they're replacing. . . . Yes I understand you would prefer new parts. But if you hadn't had the accident, new parts would have come out of your wallet, not the insurance company. We could sell you a new parts policy. But that would increase your premiums. Would you like me to have your agent quote you a new parts policy? How much more? Last time I looked it was about twenty-five percent more. No? Okay. If you're good with everything I can mail the check to your address. Or you can come by and pick it up. Today at noon? I'll have it out front. Thanks very much for your business, Mister Burris."

"Can you teach me to be that good?" Janie stands in Genevieve's cubicle entrance appearing slightly in awe of the conversation she just heard.

Genevieve nods for her to come in and sit. "You'll be as good as you want to be. That's what Janice Ramsey told me on my first day."

Janie sits down tentatively. "Janice Ramsey taught you?" Genevieve nods and Janie continues, "She still here?"

Genevieve remembers Janice and looks at Janie who could have been herself seven years ago. Genevieve remembers hoping this will be a good experience. Meanwhile dreading having to learn it all. She was also fearful of making mistakes that cost the company money and possibly her job.

The Bathroom Door

SJ sits next to Granma at the kitchen table. The older woman reads a comic book out loud. SJ keeps turning her head from side-to-side, looking at the pictures.

"And Superman lifts the runaway baby carriage into the sky as he flies back to the frightened mother." Granma reads.

SJ puts her hand over the comic. "Can I have a glass of milk, Granma?"

SJ is afraid to move, but Granma encourages her "You can get it."

"Would you get it for me?" SJ asks, not able to mask the fear in her voice.

Granma turns SJ around and looks at her. She puts her hand to SJ's forehead. "You feel okay?"

SJ nods and grabs the table to steady herself.

"No fever. Okay, let me get it for you." Granma retrieves a glass and puts it on the table.

SJ looks out of the corner of her eye before picking up the glass, takes a long drink.

"Didn't you have your milk for breakfast?" Granma asks when SJ finishes.

"We ran out. Momma forgot to buy more." SJ puts the glass back on the table.

"Your Mom's working long hours and has a lot on her mind," Granma responds as she picks up a pencil and hands it to SJ.

"Momma says you're sad." SJ wants to rest a little longer before getting back to Superman and the baby carriage rescue.

"Did she now? And why does she think I'm sad?" Granma wants to know.

"She says the bear makes you sad. But it's not the bear's fault." SJ wants her to reconsider letting her play with it.

"No, it's not the bear's fault." Granma agrees.

SJ waits, but realizes nothing more will be said. She picks up the comic book and hands it to Granma.

"Superman watches as the mother takes her baby from the carriage and he flies off to find Lex Luther to end his diabolical plot."

SJ taps the comic with her pencil.

"What is it?" Granma asks as SJ moves away.

"Bathroom." SJ utters only the single word before walking straight into the end of the open bathroom door. The impact knocks her down. She lies, dazed for a moment.

"Are you all right?" Granma flies over to her as SJ struggles to sit up, blinks her eyes, looks around and feels for the open door, just out of reach. SJ turns her head and looks out of the corner of her eye.

Granma helps her up onto her feet. "Didn't you see the door?"

"What door?" SJ responds holding her hands up as if playing blind man's bluff. Granma looks at SJ's face, "Oh, heavens. You're going to have a black-and-blue mark on your forehead. Does it hurt?"

SJ nods and feels where the bump darkens.

"Do you want to lie down?" Granma asks.

"No, I want to go to the bathroom." SJ reminds her grandmother. She keeps her hands out in front of herself, finds the bathroom door and pulls it closed behind her.

When SJ finally emerges, she still feels woozy. Hesitates before trying to cross the room. Concerned about other doors that may be hiding on her.

Granma takes her hand and guides her to the bedroom where she boosts SJ up onto the bed. "Time for a nap. Maybe you'll feel better afterwards."

"Is that door going to take a nap too, Granma?"

"I don't think so, dear."

Granma inspects the lump that forms on SJ's forehead, helps her kick off her shoes. After pulling up a light blanket, she runs her hand through her granddaughter's hair to smooth it out. "Call me if you need anything," Granma leaves the room, with the door open.

A Night at the Laundromat

Genevieve enters her mother's house in turmoil, not sure what she needs to do about her work situation, but knowing what she's doing now isn't working. When she walks into the kitchen, she finds SJ drinking a large glass of milk. That reminds her she needs to stop and pick up milk and other groceries as well on the way home. When SJ puts the glass down, the lump comes into view. "What happened?" Genevieve rushes over to the table, inspects the lump and kisses the side of her head.

SJ doesn't look directly at her, but responds, "I'm okay, Momma."

Genevieve looks up to her mother who washes dishes in the sink. "She ran into the bathroom door."

Genevieve looks back to her daughter, "Were you running around or something … not looking where you were going?"

Genevieve's mother answers for SJ, "That's the funny part. She was just going to the bathroom. She wasn't running or anything. Just said she didn't see it."

Without thinking, Genevieve puts her hand on SJ's forehead to check for fever, but doesn't detect anything. She looks at her color which seems fine. Then she inspects the lump closer. "Damn it Mom, I thought you wouldn't do this to me."

Genevieve's mother acts as if she doesn't like what she hears, "What are you saying? That I deliberately let her hurt herself?"

"You don't have to take it out on SJ, just because you're upset with me." Genevieve hears her own angry response and immediately wishes

28

she were better at not saying the first thing that comes to her mind, which she always does.

Genevieve's mother wipes her hands on the towel over her shoulder, the anger slowly builds. "I didn't *let* anything happen to my grandchild. I'm not taking anything out on her. I resent the fact you could even imagine I would do something like that."

"She's been with you almost every day for the last seven years and nothing like this ever happened before. Now you want out, so what am I to believe?" Genevieve can't let go of her suspicion. But somehow she can't believe her mother would intentionally do something like this to SJ. She turns to her daughter, "What happened, SJ?"

The little girl hugs her mother's neck. "I bumped my head."

"Didn't you see it?" Genevieve can't put it together in her own mind.

SJ shakes her head, and kisses her mother's cheek. Genevieve's mother decides to add a point. "She took a nap right after it happened and she seems fine now. Her appetite seems normal, although she's been drinking more milk than usual."

"I need to get some on the way home." Genevieve doesn't want to, but admits it.

"She told me," Genevieve's mother adds, making Genevieve want to leave.

Genevieve rises, trying to control the deep anger she feels, but suspects may not be justified. "Get your things, SJ. We need to get on home."

Genevieve's mother's hooded eyes reappear and turns back to her dishes. Genevieve steps next to her and takes the towel from her shoulder, dries dishes while she waits for SJ. "You were right."

"What about, dear?" The response from her mother sounds disinterested.

"Having too big an ego. All my hard work didn't mean a thing." Genevieve admits it, but wishes her mother wasn't right on this one. The older woman's hooded eyes go away and Genevieve can see genuine sadness in them.

SJ sits quietly in the rusted car all the way home. Finally Genevieve comes out of her thoughts and reengages with her daughter. "You feel okay?"

"You shouldn't argue with Granma."

"I wasn't arguing with her. I was just upset you got hurt." Genevieve considers her words carefully before responding.

"You tell me not to argue with you, so why do you argue with Granma?" SJ looks up at her out of the corner of her eye.

"I don't want anything bad to happen to you. When I saw this big bump in the middle of your forehead, I guess I got upset. That's all." She tries to explain, but it doesn't sound convincing even to herself.

"You argued."

"You're right. I need to be nicer to Granma." Genevieve wants to change the subject and make sure SJ really feels all right. "How do you feel?"

"Okay."

They ride on in silence for a short while, then SJ asks, "Momma, why are you so sad?"

Genevieve glances at her little girl who appears to be looking straight ahead through the windshield. "Things are difficult at work right now. I didn't get something I thought I deserved."

"Why, Momma?" SJ pushes her to give a more complete answer.

She gives it more to herself than SJ. "Because I've put myself in a box and only I can get myself out. No matter what I do, I have to change things, even if I'm the best."

"Change what, Momma?" SJ picks out the scariest word to confront.

"I have to go to night school. That means I won't be able to spend as much time with you as I do now." She knows SJ doesn't fully understand the implications.

"I don't want that, Momma. I want you to come home and be with me." SJ almost pleads in her response.

Genevieve needs to reassure SJ and herself. "It will only be for a little while. I'll spend every moment I can with you. It's just going to be less time than we have now. So that means we have to find ways to make the time we do have … special."

"Like my birthday?"

"Like your birthday, only happier than your birthday because Granma gave you a birthday spanking, as I remember," Genevieve shows a timid smile to SJ, who doesn't appear to notice.

"I don't want any more birthday spankings."

The next morning Genevieve awakens to a strange sickly sweet odor. With her eyes still half closed she stumbles out of bed, makes her way to the bathroom. A few minutes later she comes out with her eyes more wide open and her nose wrinkling at the odor. She looks around and finally decides it comes from SJ's side of the room. She goes to wake her daughter, only to be greeted by vomit in SJ's bed and covering one of the daughter's arms.

From the bathroom, she retrieves a wet washcloth and towels, and finds SJ sitting up, awake.

"What is it, Momma?" Genevieve hears the fright in the little girl's voice.

"Nothing, you just got sick in the night. I'm cleaning it up, so just lie back still until I'm done here." Genevieve reassures her as she continues cleaning up the mess. She washes her daughter's arm with the wet washcloth, dries it with a towel and then lifts her from the bed without stepping in the remaining mess.

Genevieve sends SJ off to the bathroom, but watches her walk with her arms held in front to make sure she doesn't run into something unseen. "You okay, sweetie?"

"Yes."

Genevieve notes the lack of conviction in her daughter's voice. She continues to watch her cross the room. SJ finds the door and pulls it closed behind her.

Genevieve removes the sheets and blankets, rolls them up for the Laundromat. She touches the mattress and finds the plastic casing saved it from getting wet. Genevieve dries the plastic with a paper towel, uses the wash cloth to clean it and then dries it again. "I'll stop and wash everything on the way home. While your sheets are in the dryers I'll come to Granma's and get you. How does that sound?"

SJ comes out of the bathroom, "Pick me up. We can do something special at the Laundromat, can't we?"

"Sure, we can." Genevieve isn't sure what she can do that's so special at the Laundromat, but she has the day to figure it out. SJ gets dressed as Genevieve pours her a bowl of granola for breakfast. SJ eats while Genevieve rises out the sheets, showers, gets dressed and does her morning minimal make-up routine. Never liking the heavy makeup of the older women at work, Genevieve vowed not to use any, but quickly abandoned that approach as well.

When finally ready, Genevieve emerges from the bath to find SJ sitting at the table reading a book. But the girl looks at it out of the corner of her eye. "Why are you doing that?"

"So I can read better." The matter-of-fact response catches Genevieve by surprise, as if everyone reads books this way.

"Did you eat something different at Granma's yesterday before you got sick?" Genevieve still tries to put the pieces together.

"Goat cheese."

"What did Granma make that has goat cheese in it?"

"Key ... sh." SJ sounds it out.

Genevieve thinks about it for a moment, sounds it out to herself until it finally clicks. "Oh, you mean a Quiche?"

"That's what I said, a key ... sh." And SJ is correct, that's what she said.

"We'll have to tell Granma not to use goat cheese in the future." She picks up SJ's knapsack and herds her towards the front door, scooping up the sheets and blankets on the way out.

Janie reads a training manual on line as Genevieve walks by her cubicle. "You're in early." Genevieve notes as she passes into her own cubicle, puts her purse into a drawer, locks it and adjusts the lone picture of SJ when she was about five years old.

She turns around to find Janie waiting for her. The smile doesn't appear as artificial as it did on the first day. Janie genuinely seems to be wrestling with something.

"We're really trying to balance things here, aren't we?" Janie seems hesitant, but finally asks.

"Yes. We want to pay out only the minimum we need to pay, but satisfy the customer so they'll stay with us and keep paying premiums. At the same time, we should educate them so they will have fewer claims."

"That seems contradictory." Janie muses, as if hoping Genevieve can clear it up for her.

Genevieve nods toward a chair. "During intake you get the facts, but listen to the customer, understand what they're looking for and what it will take to satisfy her or him. But during the investigation you must confirm the facts and check around to see how the claim can be settled for the lowest possible cost. The adjustment is where you bring both sides together and try to reach a middle ground that satisfies everyone as much as possible. You wear a company hat, but you're also the customer advocate in negotiations with the company. Balancing those two functions makes you successful."

Janie listens carefully and then observes, "This job's a lot harder than I thought."

"Every job is hard until you do it for a while. Just give it a chance. We're all here to help you. Pretty soon you won't think anything about it."

"When you're green you're growing and when you're ripe, you soon become rotten." Janie recites from memory.

"Where did you hear that?"

"My father said that to me when I went off to college. Said I knew all there was to know about high school. But I needed to get green again in college to make the leap to the next level." Janie pauses. "He told me the same thing when I told him I got this job."

Genevieve observes more to herself than she says to Janie, but the other woman hears it. "With you coming on board I'm going back to ripe."

"What do you mean?" Janie appears puzzled by the statement.

Genevieve doesn't want to get into this but she backed herself into a corner. "Once you're up and trained, I'll go back to being an assistant rather than continuing as an adjuster, which I've done only since Sandy left on disability. But with you on board I'll do what I've done for the past seven years, intake and investigation. Anyway, that's not your problem."

Janie struggles for a minute, and then asks, "But Allison said you were the best in the department. I should feel lucky you were going to train me. Why would they put you back into a lesser job?"

"Everyone thought Sandy was coming back. Look, it's no big deal. Not your fault. Just be the best adjuster you can be and everything will turn out fine." Genevieve wants to put this discussion to bed and get on with her work. After all, she's going to have to spend half the night in the Laundromat with SJ's sheets and blankets. *Hope they don't smell up the car too much. Probably should have washed them on the way in, but that wouldn't have worked either with me coming in so early. If this keeps up my days are going to get even longer than before.*

Janie nods to the picture of SJ. "She yours?"

Genevieve has to look around to see what Janie is referring to, sees the picture and responds, "SJ for Sarajane. Just had her seventh birthday." Comes across with pride.

"It's scary being a mother. You want the child to be perfect. Smarter than you, better looking and more successful. And when you're just starting out like I am you don't even know what that means, successful."

"You'll figure that out as you go, and so will your child."

"You're lucky, she looks like a great kid."

Genevieve looks at the picture and the devilish smile, remembering SJ had just snitched a cookie from Granma's cookie jar when the picture was taken. "She is."

Janie nods and returns to her cube as Genevieve turns on her monitor and starts her first morning routine.

Genevieve arrives at her mother's house later than usual. As she gets out of her rusting Honda, she looks up at the widow's walk and wonders if a relationship would be possible. She doesn't want to admit her mother could be right about something else too – that she just makes it harder on herself than she needs to. Having someone to share the bills with would be a big help. But most men aren't interested in high school drop outs with a kid. And those who are interested aren't the kind she would want around.

Genevieve looks at her watch as she comes into the kitchen, "I know I'm later than usual, Mom. Sorry. New girl started. I've got to train her, and it's just killing me to get my regular work done, too."

Her mother looks up at the clock on the wall. "I had plans for tonight and now it's too late for that."

"You should have said something. I could have worked things around to be here on time." She turns to SJ and gives her a big hug and kiss. "Get your things, this is laundry night."

Her mother looks at the clock again with obvious disapproval. As soon as SJ leaves the room, Genevieve moves closer to her mother. "I know this probably is a bad time to ask, but is there any way you could keep her overnight for a couple nights a week so I can go back to school?"

Her mother shakes her head. "I told you I want you to make other arrangements for her." This comes as no surprise.

"That's not practical, Mom. Without the promotion I can't add another bill. You know how tight we live. It's paycheck to paycheck. If anything unexpected happens we eat cereal for weeks." Genevieve doesn't want to give her mother more ammunition, but she doesn't know how else to convince her.

"And that's been happening more and more hasn't it?" Her mother's disapproving look causes Genevieve to turn her back. "I've given you seven years. I think that's more than you should have expected of me."

"But you love SJ as much as I do. How can you throw her out now, when she needs you, when I need you more than ever?" Genevieve realizes she isn't getting anywhere and needs to find an alternative – *but what*?

SJ enters the kitchen, walking with her head turning left and right, as if looking for something. "Are you ready, Momma?"

"Yes. Are you ready for a special night at the Laundromat?" Genevieve moves away from her disapproving mother and puts her hand on SJ's shoulder.

SJ doesn't move. "What are we going to do special, Momma?"

"I thought I'd read you a story. I got a new book from the Library today." Genevieve pushes her daughter towards the door.

"For heaven's sake, I hope it's a children's book this time." Her mother sounds annoyed even though she's won the argument.

"It's the story of a young girl and I think she'll like it."

"Pride and Prejudice?" Her mother asks.

Genevieve herds SJ out and lets the door slam without responding.

Dr. Jackson Hamilton

Genevieve makes the bed for SJ, who helps her tuck the freshly washed sheets under the mattress. SJ can't lift well. So she tucks as best she can and waits for her mother to lift the mattress. Then she pushes the sheets under. The blankets come next so Genevieve shakes them out to lie across the sheets. SJ then pulls them tight and stands back to wait for her mother to finish.

SJ collapses onto the bed.

Genevieve, thinking her little girl is just playing, pays little attention. But as she comes around the end she looks up and sees SJ seems to be shaking. Frantically, she climbs onto the mattress and hovers over her daughter, who shakes and foams at the mouth.

Put something in her mouth, she remembers, *so she doesn't swallow her tongue.* She scans the room for something … anything. Nothing comes into view. She stops to think, as hard as that is when her daughter needs help. She remembers pencils she has in her purse. She flies across the room, rips her purse open and digs through until she finds three pens, runs back to her daughter. She struggles to get SJ's mouth open, finally inserts the pens between SJ's teeth and lets her bite down on them.

Genevieve bursts into the bright lights of the Spartan hospital emergency room. "My little girl. Help me, please."

A wizened nurse sees SJ, pale and unresponsive. Her demeanor

39

changes, "Follow me, please."

The nurse motions for Genevieve to lay SJ on a gurney as she yells for a doctor.

An intern appears from the examining rooms and approaches the convulsing little girl. Her inspection takes only a moment. She wheels SJ away to an examining room as the nurse tries to calm Genevieve and direct her to the registration desk. "You need to check in over there. As soon as we know what's going on a doctor will be out to speak with you." The nurse turns to follow the intern.

Genevieve tries to comprehend the nurse's instructions, but it's as if the synapses aren't firing. She simply stands, unmoving, until the nurse turns back for a final look and points Genevieve towards the desk. Then, as if the veil lifts, Genevieve nods and moves in that direction.

After several hours in the waiting room, Genevieve dazed and half asleep, stares into space, rocks back and forth. The intern taps her on the shoulder, jarring her out of her reverie. Even so, it take a moment for her recognize the doctor.

"She's stable now." The intern appears tired, exhausted. "It was a tough one. Any seizures before or family history?"

Genevieve shakes her head.

"No, what? No seizures or no family history?"

"No seizures and only half the family history." She hates to admit this, but getting it wasn't and isn't an option.

"Father's side?"

Genevieve nods.

"What history do you have?"

Genevieve shakes her head.

"It would greatly help with the diagnosis." She flips to look at something on her chart, a puzzled expression appears and then she looks back up at Genevieve.

"Sorry, I can't get it for you." Genevieve hopes she won't ask why.

"It's really important we have a complete picture."

"Her father is dead and I have no way of reaching his family." Feelings she would rather not deal with here, rise within her and her expression hardens.

"Without the information we will need more tests. Do you really want to put her through that if they aren't absolutely necessary?"

"You'll have to do what you have to do." Genevieve is resigned.

"I'm going to admit her until we know what's going on. Who's your pediatrician?" Finishing up, her manner becomes less friendly.

"She doesn't have one." Genevieve doesn't want to get into the reasons with the doctor now as that will only make things worse.

Genevieve catches a glimpse of the look the intern gives her, and interprets it as if the intern doesn't think much of Genevieve as a mother. She doesn't visibly react to the look. After a moment the intern finally responds. "Sarajane is asleep now. I gave her a sedative that should carry her through the night. We will begin tests in the morning. The case will be assigned to Doctor Levy, a staff pediatrician since you don't have one. I suggest you go home and get some sleep. Tomorrow will be an important day for your daughter." With that short speech the intern begins to walk away.

"Wait, doctor. Can't I stay with her?"

The intern stops and shakes his head. "Not tonight. We're full and your daughter will be placed in a large pediatric ward where moms aren't allowed to stay. Sorry."

Early the next morning Genevieve flies through the Richland Insurance Company offices without stopping at her desk, even though Janie calls after her. Instead, she goes immediately to Dean's office, knocks and pokes her head in.

"Hi, Dean. I have a family health issue that came up last night." She announces then recognizes Andrea Stuart sitting across from him. "Oh, excuse me. I have to meet with the doctor again this morning to find out about some tests they're going to do. I'll make up the hours. Sorry to interrupt." Dean nods, and holds up his hand in acknowledgement; she pulls the door closed behind herself.

Really screwed that one up, didn't I? She composes herself and returns to her cubicle.

Janie waits for her, "Everything all right?"

"We'll see. What do you need?" Genevieve's mind drifts as she thinks about SJ being pushed from one lab to another, stuck with needles, tubes running medications into her veins and who knows what exotic machines and tests.

"So if you could do that for me that would be great," Janie concludes.

"What? Excuse me. Could you run that by me one more time? I'm a little distracted this morning." She hates to admit it.

Janie frowns but lets it pass. "I'd like to sit with you while you do

42

a few cases, from front to end and have you explain what you're doing and why you do it."

"Can't today as I have to get to the hospital by eight-thirty. Can you just watch me for a while? If you take careful notes, maybe in a day or two I'll get caught up and then we can do what you want." Genevieve can only see very late nights with time out for the hospital. She knows until SJ is okay, nothing else will be.

Eight-thirty comes quickly and yet it seems the morning just drags. Maybe it seems quick because she has no time to make much headway on her work, yet it drags because her mind keeps wandering back to SJ. Curious and anxious at the same time, she wonders about what SJ could be going through in the hospital.

She arrives at the waiting room, now full of couples, some clearly anxious and others appearing bored by the whole thing. She realizes she is one of the anxious ones. She needs to get that under control. A forty-ish looking and thoroughly scrubbed doctor comes through the doors and looks around. His gaze falls on Genevieve and he asks, "Misses Wilcox?"

Genevieve nods and approaches him. He extends his hand to shake hers as she reads the name on his lab coat: Dr. Jackson Hamilton. "Where's the other doctor? Doctor Levy, I think was his name," she asks the handsome doctor.

"Doctor Levy turned the case over to Doctor Grant, who's a neurosurgeon. When they completed the tests Doctor Grant asked me to come in and consult on your daughter's case, based on the preliminary results." He begins, but she cuts him off.

"What? You're the third doctor? Why didn't the first one call me when he had the preliminary results?" She's upset she hasn't been kept in the loop.

The doctor takes another breath before responding, letting her anger drop a decibel.

"Misses Wilcox."

"Miss Wilcox, I'm not married." She informs him, not completely sure why.

His expression changes as pieces of information click. "That explains the missing father's history."

She nods to confirm his guess.

"All right then. Please come to my office so we can talk in private." He motions the way. She follows his lead.

She never liked hospitals. A vague remembrance makes her uneasy and fearful that something bad is about to happen. She wonders *why that is*. But then the images return. A gurney rushes down halls. She, as a little girl, pulled along by her big father, also running. Her feet barely touch the ground as they follow the gurney. The open doors pass by with people in hospital gowns staring out at her. And then the crying. It was her mother crying. Her father was crying, too. Yet she sat in the waiting room with dry eyes, not understanding why everyone was crying.

Dr. Hamilton motions her to a chair as he closes the door and slides in behind his small cluttered desk. He puts the folder down and looks her right in the eye. "We have an MRI that suggests something that is most likely the cause of your daughter's condition. I'm a pediatric oncologist. Do you know what that means?" She has never heard the two terms used together to describe a person before. The fear of what it could mean grips her so she can't talk. She just shakes her head as that is all she can manage.

"I specialize in children with cancer. Now I know this is very hard to hear, so I'll repeat myself as many times as you want me to. SJ has a tumor. It's in her brain. We don't know how long it's been there, but I'm afraid it is advanced. It may be inoperable, but Doctor Grant wants me to see if I can shrink the tumor. If I'm successful, he may be able to remove it." He stops and waits for her to digest that information. "Do you want me to repeat any part of that?" His voice remains calm, reassuring, confident, but what he says is so unbelievable, so horrible, and so incomprehensible. *Seven year old children do not get cancer,* she screams to herself.

"Water?" It's all she can get out. The doctor pulls a small bottle from a refrigerator under his desk and hands it to her. She sips the cool liquid until half the bottle appears empty. She calms down. "How..." her scratchy voice stops her. She needs to clear her throat so she can understand herself. "How is this possible?"

"We don't really know much about the causes of pediatric cancers. But they are, unfortunately, much more common than we would like." His response seems measured and practiced to Genevieve.

"You're sure it's cancer?" She hopes this might be all speculation and maybe SJ will be all right. She just wants to take her home. But as she looks at this good-looking, confident doctor, her hopes evaporate.

"The MRI clearly shows the growth and how it impacts the surrounding brain tissues. We think this may be what caused her to walk into the door. It's probably impacting the optic nerve."

"Is my baby dying?" She can't believe the words that have come out of her mouth, but she has to know the answer.

"Survival rates in children her age are between forty and sixty percent. However, her tumor appears to be advanced.

"Can't you give me a straight yes or no?" Near tears, she struggles to hold them back.

Dr. Hamilton's response comes across both measured and

practiced. "No, but I can say this: we find cures for difficult cases. Even so, we can't predict anything with certainty."

Genevieve understands everything he says, but none of it connects as she remains in denial, hoping to find a way SJ can come home with her and be all better.

"When can she come home?"

"I can't give you a real good estimate at this time. We just don't know enough yet." Genevieve notices that he watches her eyes as he says this.

"She can't come home with me today?" Genevieve's tears are an admission she has not yet comprehended the full reality of the situation.

"No, but I can take you to see her now." He rises to show her the way.

Genevieve stops him before she steps into the hall. "Will you be her doctor through this, or do you bring in someone else now, too?" She wants some stability in a world that seems to have stopped turning.

"Doctor Grant and I will be working together on your daughter's case."

She just barely gets out the whispered, "Thank you."

The television plays cartoons, but SJ doesn't watch them. She lies back in her bed wondering where her Momma might be and why this doctor makes her do all these strange things. He seems like a nice enough man, but SJ sees sadness in his eyes and hears sadness in his voice. She wonders why he is so sad. *Momma's sad, Granma's sad. Why aren't people happy when they grow up?*

SJ sees her mother come into her room with the last doctor she's seen, Doctor Hamilton.

"Momma!" she cries and almost leaps up to hug her mother, who returns the hugs and smothers her with kisses. But something is wrong with Momma as well. *She's not happy about something. Hopefully, it's just work like before. But it sure would be nice to see her smile.*

"The doctor said you were very good through all the tests. Said you did all the things they wanted you to do like a good girl. I'm very proud of you." SJ hears her mother's words, but she still wants to know why she's not happy.

"Can we go home now, Momma?" SJ guesses at what may be the problem.

"No, kiddo. The doctors want to help you get better. They need you to stay for a while." SJ can see she was right -- *Momma is not happy about it.*

"Will you stay with me here, then?" SJ wants Momma to take her home tonight. She doesn't like this place. She wants Momma to see why she doesn't like it.

Her mother looks to the doctor who nods and responds, "We can probably accommodate you. I'll talk to the nurse." And the doctor steps out into the hall.

"I'll need to go to work tomorrow, but I'll stay today and tonight and see how it goes." Momma hugs SJ again and kisses her. A moment later a nurse comes in and goes to the chair. She pushes the back down and shows Genevieve how the chair lies out flat. "We can give you a pillow, sheets and a blanket. Won't be very comfortable, but for a night or two you'll survive."

Dr. Hamilton comes over to SJ. "Any questions before I go on and see my other patients?"

SJ shakes her head and watches her Momma. "I'm okay now."

Dr. Hamilton nods and shakes her Momma's hand, says something about talking to her in the morning and slips out the door.

"Can I have some ice cream, Momma?"

"Ice cream? Why do you want ice cream so early in the morning?"

"That nice man said I can have some any time I want."

Genevieve glances out the door as if she was going to have a word with that nice man, but he has already disappeared. "He did, did he? Well, if he said you can have it I guess you can."

"Why am I here, Momma?"

"You got sick again last night so the doctors are going to fix you up."

"Is that man the one who's going to fix me up?"

"I hope so."

Genevieve sits down on the bed next to her daughter and gives her a hug.

After dinner Genevieve gets restless. "Okay, kiddo. I need to go by the apartment, get my toiletries and a change of clothes for tomorrow. I also need to go back into work for a few hours to catch up. I'll be back before you go to sleep and I'll read you some more from the book." Her mother comes over to kiss her again.

"Do you have to go, Momma?" She pleads, but she already knows the answer. *Anyway if Momma stays the night, that's a whole lot better than waking up in this place and having all kinds of people sticking needles and running tubes and all the other things that happened today.*

"Yes, I have to go, but you can imagine what happens to Anne next and when I get back we can read and find out if you're right. How does that sound?" Momma seems happy, but there is still an undertone that worries SJ.

"All right, but don't stay too late at work or you'll be too tired and not able to stay awake." SJ admonishes her mother.

"I'll find a way to stay awake. I'm just glad…" but she doesn't finish the sentence, which seems odd to SJ. In a moment she disappears and SJ leans back to take a nap. This has been a confusing and frightening day.

That night after Genevieve finishes reading to SJ, she asks her, "How long have you had a headache?"

SJ's simple response worries Genevieve. "My head always hurts."

"Can you remember the first time your head hurt?" Genevieve fears that she should have seen this coming but didn't bother looking at the symptoms.

"No, Momma," Her response breaks Genevieve's heart.

"Do you want to talk to Granma before you go to sleep?"

"Can I call her?" SJ reaches for the phone next to the bed.

"Do you remember the number?" SJ begins dialing even before Genevieve gets the question out.

"Hi, Granma. Yes, it's me. I'm in the hospital with Momma. What am I doing here? Tests. No. They gave me tests. No, they hurt. Momma?

She's staying with me tonight." She listens to her grandmother for a moment, and then hands the phone to her mother, "She wants to talk with you."

Genevieve takes the phone, "Hi Mom, yes that's right, she's still in room eighteen-twelve in pediatrics. No, nothing more than what we talked about earlier. I don't know the answer to that, but let me ask the doctor when he comes by in the morning. I remembered what I wanted to ask you earlier. Do you remember SJ talking about her head hurting? You know, headaches or anything like that? No? And she never had a problem seeing until she walked into the door? No? Oh. Okay. No everything's under control. Yes, I'm staying here tonight with her. If you could stop by tomorrow I'm sure she would like that. You should check with the nurse's station first or you may have to wait for her to come back from the treatments they're giving her. No, I don't know when they are going to do that. I'm not sure everything is scheduled yet." Genevieve listens to her mother for a while, and then has only one final comment, "Yes, I do remember it. Night, Mom, I'll call you tomorrow."

She puts the receiver back into the cradle, gives SJ final hugs and kisses and then crawls into her makeshift bed turning out the light, "Night kiddo. Another adventure coming tomorrow."

SJ responds with, "I hope there aren't any more needles. They hurt."

The Story of Bearmas

A very tired-looking but showered and dressed Genevieve sits on the bed next to her daughter. Genevieve's hair remains wet. Make-up has not been added yet. But SJ listens, enthralled by the story her mother tells. "And that's how the lion found its tail."

SJ doesn't want her mother to leave yet. "One more, this time about a bear."

"A bear, huh? Let me see…" Genevieve tries to think of a story. As she thinks about it, the forty-ish Dr. Hamilton steps to the door but stops to listen.

"Well … did I ever tell you the story of Bearmas?"

Genevieve doesn't want to get into another discussion about the attic bear that Genevieve's mother will not let SJ play with. She tries to make this one up as she goes. She already told SJ all the bear stories she knows at least a million times, or so it seems.

"No, tell me." An eager smile appears on SJ. Genevieve smiles back, happy to see her daughter excited as her imagination goes to work.

"Well the celebration of the birth of a bear is called Bearmas."

"Why isn't it just a birthday?" SJ asks her mother.

"There's more to the story. Just listen." Genevieve responds.

"Okay."

"Did you know that when little girls and boys need help or comfort, that a bear is born? That bear is intended for that little boy or girl and no one else." As Genevieve begins to tell it, the story begins to flow.

"Like me?" SJ gets more excited envisioning her own bear.

"Yes, just like you." Genevieve kisses her daughter on the top of her head.

"Now that bear has to prove to its parents and the Supreme Bear Council that it's worthy of being the one special bear for that little boy or girl. In order to do this the bear must undergo a whole series of ordeals to prove it."

"What's worthy mean?" SJ tries to take this all in.

"Worthy is when you show that you deserve something. Like I was worthy of promotion at work. But it looks like Andrea didn't agree." Genevieve reflects and SJ gets impatient with her.

"Stick to the bear, Momma. So what's an ordeal?"

"An ordeal is something very difficult to accomplish. It's very hard to get through, because there are all kinds of unpleasant things that happen. Ordeals generally aren't much fun."

"Did you ever have an ordeal, Momma?" SJ asks, wondering.

"You don't have ordeals; you endure them. They take a long time."

"Longer than a movie?" SJ asks trying to understand.

"Much longer." Genevieve responds.

"That's a long time. Can you pause it in the middle to go to the bathroom?"

"Let's get back to the story. Okay?" Genevieve doesn't want to get sidetracked.

SJ glances up at her mother but does not respond.

"All right, now let me see. The bear has to undergo a series of ordeals."

"What's a series?" SJ isn't going to let her mother not tell her what she needs to know.

"More than one."

"How many is that?" SJ wonders aloud.

"I'm not sure. Ten, maybe."

"But if ordeals take a long time, when do I get my bear?" SJ sees the outcome she wants.

"When your bear has completed them … his ordeals."

"But I want my bear now." Comes across almost as a cry.

"I know, honey, but you'll have to wait. Can I finish the story now?"

SJ sulks as she listens.

"Some bears don't succeed in all of their ordeals."

"Is that why I don't have a bear?"

"I don't know sweetheart." Genevieve responds wondering.

"What happens if he doesn't succeed?"

Genevieve reaches for an answer, and one appears. "The bear becomes disgraced and must join the salmon hunters, also known as the redeeming bears.

"What's redeeming?" SJ wonders aloud.

"If you don't do something right, you can redeem yourself by doing something to show you are worthy."

"How does my bear redeem?" SJ isn't going to stop until she understands.

Doctor Hamilton enters the room and sits down on the chair to listen. Genevieve gets up, but he motions for her to continue.

"How does my bear redeem, Momma?"

Genevieve hesitates for a moment, with an unexpected audience. She tries to collects her thoughts, distracted by the good-looking doctor. She's not sure she likes having an audience for the rest of this. She also knows she's keeping the doctor from his rounds.

"For a year the redeeming bear must fish for salmon."

"What are salmon?"

"They're big fish found in the most remote rivers of Alaska." Genevieve responds.

"And why does he have to fish there?"

"To feed all of the northern bear tribes." Is the simple response.

"One bear has to feed all the other bears? That doesn't sound fair." SJ observes, trying to understand this story.

"It gets worse. At the end of that year each redeeming bear must then join the baklava bakers." Genevieve explains.

"What's a baklava?"

"You've had them. They're those little squares I sometimes bring home from the bakery. They're made from nuts and honey and phyllo dough. You like them."

"Can you bring me a baklava?" SJ asks remembering the sweet treat.

"Tomorrow. Now let me finish. So the redeeming bears must gather nuts and honey and make baklava for all of the northern bear tribes."

"Can I be a northern bear?" SJ asks, wondering what the rules are.

"Why would you want to be a northern bear?" her mother responds.

"If I'm not going to get one, maybe I should be one." SJ laughs.

Genevieve hugs her daughter. "Sorry. You are what you are. Besides, it gets very cold in the far north and you don't like the cold. You told me yourself."

SJ shudders, thinking about the cold.

"After a year making baklava they have redeemed themselves. They become eligible to challenge the ordeals for their chosen boy or girl. But this must be their last chance."

"Last chance? What happens to them?" This thought upsets SJ.

"If the redeemed bear successfully makes it through the ordeals, they come and live with their chosen boy or girl. But if the bear fails at even one ordeal, it finds itself cast out of the bear tribes. It must then wander the wilderness of the most far northern reaches of Alaska."

"That's very sad." SJ observes.

"But think about it. Bears can be small or very big."

"Why is that?"

"Smaller bears successfully complete all their ordeals. But if a much larger bear arrives, then you know that bear didn't make it through the first time, but is a redeemed bear."

"Why is it bigger?" SJ wonders aloud.

"From eating all the salmon and baklava."

"I don't want a redeemed bear." SJ isn't sure she likes this story.

"If you think about it, though, redeemed bears have many more stories to tell and are also good salmon fishermen and baklava bakers. That's why when we celebrate Bearmas, we always eat salmon and baklava in remembrance of the redeeming bears."

SJ's eyes become wide, "Then that bear in the attic must have passed its ordeals the first time because it was a small bear."

"Yes, and was polite and minded its manners, as I remember." Genevieve does not want to stop now, but looks at her watch and starts to get up, until SJ pulls her back down. "So when is Bearmas, Momma?"

"Bearmas can be anytime a boy or girl needs a bear. We don't actually celebrate the day the bear is born, because we don't know if it will pass its ordeals. So Bearmas is a celebration of that bear's birth on the day it passes the last of its ordeals and arrives to live with the chosen boy or girl. Does that make sense?" Genevieve glances at her watch. She becomes embarrassed at how long it took to tell the story and how late she will be for work.

Then Dr. Hamilton speaks up. "That was a wonderful story about Bearmas. I'd never heard it before. But Sarajane, you don't have a bear? Why --?"

SJ cuts him off, "SJ. My name is SJ. People only call me Sarajane when I've done something bad."

"Excuse me, SJ. Why don't you have a bear?"

"He must be going through his ordeals." SJ realizes aloud.

"And the ordeals are very dangerous. But I'm sure your bear is very smart, courageous and brave and will succeed." Dr. Hamilton adds.

SJ ask Dr. Hamilton, "What happens to the boy or girl if their bear is cast out of the Northern Bear tribes?"

"As I understand it, the Supreme Bear Council selects another bear. And that's why sometimes boys and girls wait a long time to get their bear. Now let's take a look at you." The doctor eases into the examination, and Genevieve pulls the door shut.

The Glass Cactus

Neon lights fill the Glass Cactus nightclub. A big dance floor and stage for local cover bands that start playing at nine fills the room. Dr. Hamilton arrives at seven, and waits at the bar for the tall and very attractive Michele Franklin. He has settled into a funk. Michele seems to be the only person who usually brings him back out. He knows he needs a dose of reality therapy. As the Chief Financial Officer for a publicly traded company, Michele deals with reality and 'telling it like it is' every day.

They met at a birthday party for his partner. Dated off and on for over a year. They like many of the same things. Enjoy traveling and exploring the world. But also see very different things in art and like totally different music. A standing joke between them has been that they always tend to go to a club rather than a restaurant, even though one or the other will probably hate the band.

Recently he finds himself wondering whether she might be the one. Sure, they have fun every time they do something together. And while he is very attracted to her, he has held back and not made a physical commitment to the relationship.

He wonders if he hasn't waited too long now to start a family. His partners come in with stories of their children's Little League and Pop Warner exploits. But something has always held him back. He thinks it's the same reason he has periodic funks ... depressions ... but he won't admit that to himself or anyone else, not even to Michele. But he can see in her eyes that she knows ... understands what he's going through. He suspects she has them too. Or possibly a family member suffers from them. Either way, she recognizes the symptoms.

While he thinks about this, the long legs and flowing red hair come through the doorway. Every head in the club turns to appreciate her. He follows the eyes to her to be greeted by a smile that melts him every time. Dr. Hamilton does not wait, but crosses the room to meet her. She rewards him with a kiss that lasts a little longer than he intended, but he doesn't complain.

He feels the male stares in the club falling away first, as the men realize she is taken. The female eyes remain, however. Dr. Hamilton surmises they are trying to puzzle out whether they're as ideal as they appear. The eyes follow them as they walk together to the bar.

Her Grey Goose Martini waits for her at the bar next to his Dewar's and water. But the drinks remain untouched for much of the conversation. "How was your board meeting?" he asks to start a conversation about her rather than about himself.

"Exhausting as usual. We prepared thoroughly. They accepted our recommendations. So now all we have to do is execute the plan." As she responds, she looks into his eyes. He sees something troubles her.

"You make business sound so simple." He wants to keep it going, hoping she will give him another discourse on the complexity of the business environment or some such aspect of what she does all day.

But she surprises him with her response, "Not so different from what you do. You and I both deal with unknowns, make judgments and hope for the best as we put our plans into effect. Hopefully, we learn from the mistakes of others before we make them ourselves. But in the end, we can only do our best. So, why are you depressed?"

Uncomfortable, Dr. Hamilton shifts about in his chair. "I may be in a funk, but I'm not depressed."

"The clinician who denies a diagnosis." She points out the folly of his avoidance. He wants to run away. Yet, he needs to stay or it will only get worse.

"Why aren't you a doctor?" He kids her, already knowing the

answer.

"Because I intend to marry one." Her response jars him, taking his thoughts down a much unexpected lane.

"Anyone I know?" He volley's back.

"Apparently not very well." It slams into him like an overhead smash that causes him to sip his Dewar's.

"Grey Goose Martini, the way you like it." He points to her drink, hoping to find a little more time to think of another topic.

"Alcohol isn't good for you, especially when you're dep . . ., when you're in a funk. You tell me that all the time. So what did you really want to talk about since it doesn't involve marriage?"

He can see her backing away from him. It makes him afraid that if he doesn't do something quickly, she will get up and leave. "A seven year old…" he begins, but she doesn't wait.

"And you don't think you can save her. You know you should have been a preacher. Then you could claim to save folks without having to prove it with objective evidence."

"Must have been some board meeting." He makes the observation hoping to buy a little more time to come up with a new topic.

"Why is every kid you see a manhood test for you? It's like every three months you call me up and want me to pull you back out of the black hole you live in. You need to change specialties or figure out how to be happy with what you do for the kids you save." She frowns as he takes a second sip of Dewar's. A moment later she rises and troops off to the ladies room. To cool off, he suspects.

He looks around the club, observes the expressions on the others there. Most are smiling or laughing about something, telling stories to entertain and make the other person happy. And all he's done is piss off this gorgeous, intelligent woman who cares for him. *Kids get cancer and some die. Adults get cancer and a whole lot more of them die. So why can't I just apply what I've learned and not take it so personally?*

Michele returns from the ladies room with that same sexy walk. But her expression conveys her unhappiness. Dr. Hamilton pushes the drink away, stands up to welcome her back. "Sorry. Can we put away the shingle for a while and talk about something fun?"

He sees the flicker of interest in her eyes, but also knows her mouth still waits for the kisses she came for. "I've been thinking of going to Santiago, Chile for a long weekend."

"What's in Santiago?" she asks neutrally.

"One of my partners went down a few months ago with his wife and some friends. They did tours and wine samplings at some of the vineyards and had a great time. He raved about how you fly overnight and don't get jet lagged because you don't cross many time zones," He relaxes as he recounts the story.

"Could be fun. What else did he say?" He hears the unwillingness to have expectations. He realizes she wants to be woo-ed.

"Charlie's the one who went. Anyway, he said they hired this guide . . . name's Mauricio. He drove them everywhere. Took them to fabulous restaurants where he ordered platters of different kinds of foods. Charlie talked about razor clams -- he called them. Anyway, they serve them on the half shell, baked with parmesan cheese and a little milk. He said his wife loved them. Everything was so good -- and inexpensive, when you compare it to Europe and the Euro." He sees that piques her interest. But still she waits and he knows time is running out.

"So, Charlie said that once Mauricio figured out the kinds of wine they liked best, he got on his cell and rearranged their whole itinerary. Took them to other wineries they liked even more. He said that each day they were there they enjoyed better food and better wines. It just got better and better. I'm asking you if you would go with me." *There, I got it out.*

He suspects she considers what a trip with him could be like. Then he notices the window close again. He suspects she considers what it might really be like. "I'm looking to marry a doctor. Will this trip bring me any closer to my goal?"

The bells in his head scream. *This is the break or make point in this relationship.* He knows he can't expect her to continue the relationship unless he makes a commitment to her right here and now.

"I want you to come to Santiago with me, just the two of us." *Seems safe, a step in the direction she wants, but not setting the date.*

"And?"

Whoops, not good enough. "…and when we come back … we should … know." He tries to say what she wants to hear, and he knows this could blow up in his face; but he simply can't say the words. He looks at her mouth. He sees the lips tighten. He closes his eyes expecting her to walk out. Instead she leans over and kisses him with those lips … those expectant lips … and she holds that kiss.

"Is that a yes?" His mind suddenly questions what she meant. Yes or goodbye. But he knows that was no goodbye kiss.

"When?" The mouth invites him back, but the eyes still wait for the commitment.

"As soon as you can get away?" He makes the offer, but she still waits for something more.

"How long have I known you? About a year and a half. And I haven't seen you take a single day of vacation in all that time. You always have patients who need you more than I do, or so you think. I want you to hand me both our tickets tomorrow. Even then I don't expect it to happen." She picks up the Grey Goose Martini. Considers it for a long moment, then drinks it all in a single motion.

"So this is the test. Am I willing to change for you?" He puts the question on the table to see what it takes to resolve the situation.

"I've heard a lot of words in the last eighteen months. But your actions tell me something else. I deal in objective evidence. You haven't shown me any." He stares at the Dewar's as he considers both what she says and the tone of the words.

When he turns back to her, those lips are parted ever so slightly, waiting in anticipation. He can see her eyes are betting he will not follow through. He knows at that instant what he needs to do. *But are you really ready for this, now? She's no virgin, but you still are. If you don't perform that will be the end.* He finally expresses his fears to himself. But those parted lips are so inviting, waiting for him, saying yes, now, end the waiting.

"Your place or mine?" He asks and sees her lips part a little more. The surprise in her eyes.

"You've never even been to my place." She notes.

"Maybe now's a good time to find out if I like your decorator."

Sick

The next morning Dr. Hamilton comes to SJ's room to find the little girl with a book open on her lap. But she doesn't seem to be reading it. "Good morning, sunshine. How do you feel today?" He knows from the treatments that she won't feel well at all. But he wants her to tell him that.

"Sick." She says no more.

"Where do you feel sick?"

"Stomach mostly." She appears lethargic.

"Feel kind of weak? No energy?" She nods but does not answer. "That's normal from the medication we gave you yesterday. You'll feel better tomorrow. It will get better every day." The Santiago story comes back to mind, but he knows that means something else entirely in this situation "Let me check your breathing."

She leans forward so he can listen through his stethoscope. She does so and projectile vomiting covers the breakfast and bed.

"Oops, let me get someone from housekeeping in here to clean that up." He picks her up out of the mess. Goes to the bathroom for a washcloth. As he opens the door, he finds Genevieve there, covering big, dark circles under her eyes with makeup. "Little accident here. Can you hand me the washcloth?" Genevieve looks at SJ and at the vomit on her face, on her hands, everywhere. She then remembers the washcloth and rinses it out for him.

Together, they clean her up, and then sit SJ down in the chair, the same chair Genevieve sleeps on.

He goes to the intercom and presses the button. "This is Doctor Hamilton, can you have housekeeping stop by room eighteen twelve and change a bed for me, as soon as possible?"

"Yes doctor." Comes over the intercom.

Dr. Hamilton then approaches SJ. "Shall we try this once more?" He puts the stethoscope into his ears and listens to her breathe.

Genevieve watches with apprehension. The odor of the vomit reaches her. She wiggles her nose in recognition, checks her watch. "I need to get into work."

Dr. Hamilton takes the cue and steps aside so she can give her daughter a kiss and hug for the day.

"Are we going home today, Momma?" SJ asks once she has her arms around her mother's neck.

"What do you think?"

"I feel sick," SJ responds.

"Best place to be when you're sick is the hospital, isn't it? And you have the nice Doctor Hamilton here looking out for you to make sure you're getting better." She tries to sound reassuring.

"Do you know what ordeal my bear is going through today, Momma?" SJ asks without any energy, although she can't hide worrying about it. "I hope he completes them soon so I can have my bear."

Dr. Hamilton answers first, "You know SJ, we don't get to see the ordeals when they happen. But if you want I'll stop by tonight when your Momma gets back from work. I'm sure together we can tell you about the first ordeal." He winks at a surprised Genevieve, who takes a minute to recover.

"That sounds good, doesn't it?" Genevieve responds as she studies

Dr. Hamilton. He tries to exude confidence, even though he can't even begin to think what an ordeal would need to entail.

SJ doesn't want to wait, but the resignation comes across in her voice. "All right. But it better be a great story."

"I'll ask the other doctors about the ordeals their kids' bears went through. Maybe we can figure it out," Dr. Hamilton volunteers. Genevieve nods to him.

"Bye honey. You feel better." She kisses SJ and hurries on her way.

Insurance

Genevieve receives a call at work from the hospital business office. During her lunch hour, she walks into the tiny office of the accounts receivable clerk, Natalie Ross, a friendly middle-aged woman.

"Misses Wilcox, I've been reviewing your insurance and the bills you're running up. I think we need to talk about them now." The older woman states as she pulls up the information on her computer screen.

"Let me see … hmmm … here we are. It says your insurance requires a deductible of three thousand dollars…."

"Three thousand dollars!" Genevieve had no idea of her financial obligation.

"That's not all; you have a co-insurance on the next three thousands of twenty percent, but everything above that your insurance covers at one-hundred percent. That's the good news."

"Good news? So you're saying what? That I have to pay three thousand, then twenty percent of the next three thousand? That's three thousand, six hundred dollars!" Genevieve tries to take this all in. "I thought the insurance would pay for all of it."

"Heavens no. You actually have very good insurance coverage. I'm sure you know you'll have doctor and hospital bills and you'll have to pay something toward them. You also have to meet the deductible every year."

Genevieve doesn't answer, doesn't tell she didn't know all this.

"Since you work at an insurance company ... at least, according to your records ... I'd think you'd know all this," Natalie responds.

"I don't do medical, just the property and casualty side of the business." She tries to think what she can do. After a few moments she looks up at Natalie. Slowly shakes her head, "I don't know what to do. I can't pay thousands of dollars. I can't even buy my little girl a stuffed bear."

"I thought that might be the case. What we can do is put you on a payment plan, so much every week. That keeps it out of collections," Natalie offers.

"Collections? Oh, no. If the company found out that I had a collections agency after me I'd lose my job," Genevieve rambles on in a panic.

"It's okay, dear. That's why we do the installments. Now if you want I can work with your doctors and the pharmacy on their payments and set up a single payment account for you,"

"Yes, please." Genevieve thinks for a few moments then realizes she needs a key piece of information. "How much will you be looking for in payments?"

"At least a hundred a week. With the bills you're running up that will take you several years to pay back."

Genevieve can't imagine paying for so long and shakes her head.

"Oh, and at the rate your bills are running, we'd like you to make the first payment before the end of the month." Natalie's friendliness disappears. A frown appears to indicate an end to the meeting. Natalie rises and so does Genevieve, as if on autopilot.

THE FIRST BEARMAS

Granma comes by the hospital, looking lost and apprehensive about what she will find. The short gray-haired nurse on the floor points her towards SJ's room. But Granma peeks inside before entering.

SJ hears the familiar Granma sounds, her walk and her sudden sighs. "Granma!" SJ holds her arms up for her but does not get out of bed, nor does she look directly at her.

"Some fancy hotel they've put you up in. What did you do to warrant this?"

Granma coming to keep her company, and the familiar smells and touches make her feel better. "I got sick, Granma."

"That's what your mother said on the phone." Granma looks SJ over. "But you look fine to me. I think you should come to Granma's house and we can have a tea party. How does that sound?"

SJ feels sad, rather than happy. "I can't Granma. Momma says the hospital is where I need to be until I'm better. An' Doctor Hamilton says I'll feel a little better every day."

"I hope so, child. This is no place for you. We have things to do and places to see and people to talk with...."

But SJ cuts the discourse short. "Who, Granma? Who do we need to go see?"

"Lots of people. Like the neighbors, and people at church, and your great Aunt Bridgette..."

Dr. Hamilton walks by and hears the voices in SJ's room. He stops to look in. "But why not the bear, Granma? The one in the attic. Is the Gestapo coming for him too? Is that why you won't let him out?" SJ bursts into tears.

"Gestapo? What are you talking about?"

SJ sniffles. "Momma's reading me the story of the girl who lives in her attic. Anne."

Granma sounds bewildered. "What is your mother reading to you?"

Dr. Hamilton interrupts. "Everything all right here?"

"Oh, yes. I'm SJ's Granma. Everything's fine."

"SJ's mother spoke of you. What's the problem with the bear?" His curiosity aroused.

"Nothing really. You know how children get fixated on things."

He puts on his best clinical voice. "What do you mean, fixated?"

Granma's voice betrays her anxiety, "It's a private matter between my granddaughter and me."

Dr. Hamilton nods but appears even more curious than before. He looks over at SJ and reminds her, "Doctor Coolidge told me an ordeal I think you'll enjoy, SJ."

"Really? Tell me now." Still in bed, she gets up onto her knees and tries to see the doctor, looking out of the side of her eye.

Observing this behavior, Dr. Hamilton steps closer and moves his hand directly in front of her. "Do you see my hand?"

SJ turns her head, looks at a right angle toward the doctor. "There it is."

"Do you know what Pirates are, SJ?

"Of course. Momma read me Treasure Island." She responds as if everyone's Momma did that.

"Well, I'm making you a pirate. He takes a juvenile eye patch from his pocket and puts it over her right eye.

"When I'm better could I put this patch on my Bear's eye to make him a pirate?" she asks hopefully.

"What if your bear's a girl?" he asks.

"I'm a girl and I have a patch."

"You're right. So if your bear's a girl bear she could still be a pirate."

Granma watches this whole thing. Seems unsure of what to make of it. But she finally asks, "Why can't she see in her right eye?"

Dr. Hamilton tugs the eye patch down just a little and turns to Granma. "She has pressure behind the eye. We're trying to reduce that pressure with the current treatment. If we're successful she should regain her sight."

"And how long do you think that will take?" Granma seems skeptical.

"We don't know -- Misses Wilcox, is it?"

Granma nods. "Why don't you know?"

"We're dealing with a moving target. Every time we think we know something absolutely, we find that we know nothing, absolutely."

"Double talk. All you doctors are the same." She dismisses him.

"I take it you don't like doctors much." He gives her an opening to express what she really thinks, but she doesn't take it.

"I hope you realize doctors are just people. There are good doctors and doctors who aren't as good. We all want to help as much as we're able. But disease and injury are things that are governed by the human body. Not even the most skillful doctor can cure everyone. In the end we're only human."

Granma looks at Dr. Hamilton, but says nothing more to him.

He gets the message, "I'll see you tonight, SJ. Make sure your mother has the nurse call me when she gets here. We have serious storytelling to do." Dr. Hamilton says, winks and then leaves them.

"Is the Gestapo going to take him away?" SJ demands of her grandmother.

"The doctor?" Granma seems confused.

"No, the bear in your attic." SJ tries to get some answers to questions that have haunted her all day

The First Ordeal: The Burning Bridge

Genevieve arrives, windblown and looking extremely tired. She finds SJ sits on her bed with the patch over her right eye and a book on her lap. Genevieve hangs up the clothes for the next day then tries to put her hair back into place before she kisses SJ.

"You a pirate?"

"Doctor Hamilton gave me this. Said I could give it to my bear when he comes."

"So you think you're getting a bear, do you?" Genevieve shakes her hair out. She tries to figure out how to get her daughter a bear – while paying the hospital one hundred dollars a week. And god only knows how much to a child caregiver now that her mother is abandoning them. "You may be waiting a while, you know."

"That's okay. My bear has to undergo ordeals to get to me."

"And that bear's ordeals are just like the ones we all go through from time to time." Genevieve thinks about her daughter's ordeal.

"Doctor Hamilton said you should make sure the nurse calls him." SJ reminds her mother. Genevieve instantly gets flustered and heads for the bathroom to make sure she looks all right.

"Why are you doing that, Momma? It's not morning."

"Just because, kiddo." She puts her hair back together and checks her make-up. "I look so old."

"What's wrong with looking old, Momma? You are old."

73

Dr. Hamilton comes into the room with a smile for SJ.

"Thanks a lot. If Doctor Hamilton comes in, would you let me know?" Genevieve works to put everything back into place.

Before SJ can respond, Dr. Hamilton places his finger to his lips. He walks softly to the bathroom door. "Why do I always find you here?" he asks.

Genevieve jumps with a start, causing her hair to fall apart. She blows a hanging strand out of her eye. To no avail. She hangs it over her ear.

"You look fine, come on, SJ wants to hear her first bear ordeal." Dr. Hamilton takes her hand, gingerly.

Genevieve experiences a shock from his touch as he leads her out of the bathroom.

"The doctor said he would tell me about the first ordeal." SJ reminds them both.

Dr. Hamilton sits on SJ's bed, "Do you like our pirate?" He asks Genevieve.

She nods before responding, "Very becoming."

Dr. Hamilton stops for a moment as if to remember. "Doctor Coolidge told me this story just this morning. It seems there was this bear named Ralph. He was selected for a little girl, very much like our SJ here, by the Supreme Bear Council. Now he was told by the Grizzly bear chairman of the council that Ralph has to successfully overcome many Ordeals before he joins his little girl at her Bearmas. Anyway, the Polar Bear who is the Master of Ordeals, pulls a ball from the great Ordeal Mixer that is a lot like one of those lottery machines that has the balls with the numbers on them...."

"She's never seen that." Genevieve lets the doctor know so he won't belabor it.

SJ corrects her mother. "Yes I have. I saw a woman in black pajamas turn on this machine. It had balls that flew through the air. She did something and one of the balls rolled out. It had a number on it."

"Well the Great Ordeal Mixer is a lot like that. Only when the ball comes out it has an ordeal written on a slip of paper inside the ball. So back to our story. When the Master of Ordeals opens the ball and reads the ordeal to Ralph --"

"What was his first ordeal?" SJ interrupts impatiently.

"The Master of Ordeals read the slip of paper that says only, 'Cross the Bridge of Fire.' Every bear gasped in horror for no bear ever returned from this dreaded ordeal."

SJ gazes off into the distance as if picturing a burning bridge in her mind's eye.

"Well anyway," the doctor continues, "Ralph looks to his father and says, 'I cannot do this. No bear has ever survived the Bridge of Fire.' And Ralph's father looks at his son and says, 'I raised you to do what is right and what is important. You have a little girl that waits for you to prove yourself worthy of her. I believe you are worthy for you are my son. I believe that you will find a way to cross the Bridge of Fire and come back to us. I have taught you many lessons. But the most important lesson is to believe in yourself and to use your imagination to solve problems. I will wait for your safe return.'"

"His father really loves him, doesn't he?" SJ asks with a tear in her eye.

"Yes, he does. But not just his father. Ralph turns to his mother and says, 'Mother I cannot do this. No bear has ever survived the Bridge of Fire.' And Ralph's mother hugs her son and says simply, 'Your father and I believe in you.'"

SJ asks, "Can't they give him a magical weapon?"

Dr. Hamilton replies, "They could, but since his parents aren't magicians, they have none to give him."

SJ appears to think about that for a moment. She finally looks to her mother and says, "So how does he get across the Bridge of Fire?"

Dr. Hamilton continues, "So the Master of Ordeals gives Ralph directions to find the Bridge of Fire. Ralph the Bear starts down the road with only the fur on his back and a smile on his face."

SJ interrupts again, "And what color is his fur?"

Dr. Hamilton has to think a moment. "Hmmm. Doctor Coolidge didn't say, but he must have been a brown bear."

"Why?" SJ demands impatiently.

"As a black bear he could sneak up on the Bridge of Fire in the night and cross it in the dark. The Bridge wouldn't even knowing he was there. But that's not the way it happened, according to Doctor Coolidge."

"Okay." SJ accepts that explanation.

Dr. Hamilton notices an expression on Genevieve that makes him think she is wondering how she will match this story.

"So Ralph follows the path to the dreaded Bridge of Fire. Along the way he comes across a farmer putting shingles on his barn. The farmer appears old and tired. The farmer asks Ralph for help with the shingles. The farmer explains the fall will soon be upon them. The rains will ruin the hay if he doesn't have the roof finished. Ralph the Bear was taught to do only right and important things. He decides to help the farmer. So he stays for three days carrying up and nailing shingles onto the roof. Then on the third night the rains come. But the roof is complete and the hay saved."

SJ becomes impatient. "So he's just putting off going to the bridge like I put off going to bed."

Dr. Hamilton smiles at her admission then contradicts her. "No, he did what was right and what was important. It was right to help the farmer. It was important that the hay be saved to feed the livestock through the winter. But anyway, the farmer asked Ralph how he could repay his kindness? Ralph tells him that he has to cross the Bridge of Fire as part of his ordeals to become worthy of his little girl. The farmer thinks for a minute and says, 'I know a way. Let me help you.' So the farmer goes to his barn and builds a wheel, a big wheel, as tall as I am, all made of wood."

"What good is a wheel?" SJ wants to know, confused.

"Just listen. He puts shingles around the rim of the wheel and a door into one side. He stands the wheel up on end and tells Ralph, 'If you get inside this wheel at the entrance to the bridge and run inside it so you cross very quickly, I think you will make it.' Ralph looks at the wheel. He asks why the farmer thinks this will protect him?

"The farmer responds, 'Three reasons: one is by helping me for three days it's now the rainy season and the fire has died down; so it's not as hot. Second, the shingles that will touch the surface of the bridge are made of asbestos and burn very slowly; that will give you more time. And third, if you run very quickly, the fire won't have a chance to burn the wood of the wheel.'"

Sounding confused, SJ asks, "Isn't that cheating? The farmer's helping him."

Dr. Hamilton smiles again. "No, SJ. It's always better to make friends. They can help solve your problems. No one can solve every problem all alone."

SJ falls silent, as if thinking, then suddenly says, "Okay."

Dr. Hamilton continues the ordeal. "So the farmer helps Ralph roll the wheel to the dreaded Bridge of Fire. When they arrive, Ralph becomes frightened and says to the farmer, 'If this is what the fire is like when low, I can't imagine what it's like when it's not the rainy season.'

And the farmer tells the bear, 'In the summer even this wheel wouldn't be fast enough to save you. But now with courage and your greatest effort you can make it.' So Ralph opens the door, climbs in and starts walking the wheel towards the bridge. The farmer sees that he goes too slowly. He yells at the bear, 'Faster! Faster!' Ralph hears the farmer's calls. He runs inside the circle. He runs faster and faster. Faster even than he has run in his whole life. And when the wheel hits the dreaded Bridge of Fire, he runs so fast that the flames can't burn the wood. The temperature inside the wheel rises so high the bear sweats. The sweat gets in Ralph's eyes, stinging them. He slows as he wipes the sweat away. As he starts running faster again, sweat pours into his eyes once more. Again he slows to wipe away the moisture that makes it difficult for him to see where he's going. He picks up the pace again, wiping his eyes as she goes. He fears that he still has a long way to go. But then, he feels the temperature dropping, feels the wheel slowing even with his extra effort. He realizes he has started up hill on the other side of the bridge."

"Wow, he did it." SJ rejoices.

Dr. Hamilton puts up his hand to caution her not to celebrate just yet. "But wait. Ralph realizes he is now on the wrong side of the bridge. He has to walk for many days to get home. So do you know what that silly little bear did?"

Again appearing confused, SJ shakes her head.

"He starts running backwards, so the wheel will cross back over the bridge, going in the opposite direction. The farmer shouts at him not to try this. It's much too dangerous. But Ralph can only think about completing this ordeal. He wants to get to his little girl sooner. So he runs as hard and fast as he can backwards. But if you've ever run backwards, you know you're slower than when you're going forwards.

So, the wheel rolls much slower back across the bridge. Soon, it becomes much hotter. Ralph sweats. The sweat pours into his eyes again so that he can't see where he is going. The fire singes the wood. It burns with clouds of smoke. And still Ralph has crossed only half of the bridge. So do you know what that bear did?"

SJ and Genevieve both shake their heads 'no'.

"He stops the wheel in the middle of the bridge. He turns around inside it. And then he runs again. This time he runs forward as fast as he can. As he reaches the other side, the farmer tosses a pail of water on the burning wood. He quickly opens the door so Ralph the Bear can hop out. Ralph is saved with only singed fur around his ankles."

Genevieve smiles at Dr. Hamilton and says, "So the bear passes his first ordeal."

SJ responds, "Yes, twice."

Dr. Hamilton nods, but completes the story.

"The bear was so grateful he decides not to rush home. He stays for another few days to help the farmer build a new chicken coop. 'Thank you, thank you,' says the farmer. 'Now I can raise more chickens.'

"Ralph adds, 'And have more eggs.'

"The farmer thinks for a moment and realizes, 'And have more to eat during the cold, cold winter.' The farmer smiles and pats his round, fat tummy.

"Ralph smiles at the happy farmer and decides. 'Yes, definitely, I'll stay.

'Then we must celebrate,' says the farmer, so he and the bear prepare a picnic. They invite the chickens to celebrate, and the frogs from the pond, and the bluebirds that nest in the big elm tree. All the rabbits say they'll come. As do the possums and the raccoons. And the little brown mice that live snuggled in the hay in the barn. The farmer doesn't invite the skunk, but he doesn't raise a stink.

The picnic is a big success. Ralph has more fun than he's ever had before. The blue birds sing while the raccoons and rabbits join in. The little brown mice hold hands with the frogs and dance around the bond fire. The farmer can't stop laughing, his big, round tummy shaking like Jell-O. Neither can Ralph stop laughing, for we all know how much fun bears have at picnics."

"I think I'm past the barnyard animals." SJ informs the doctor.

"Well ...that was how he repaid the kindness the farmer showed him. Then he went home to his mother and father. When they saw him with only slightly singed fur, his mother said, 'We believe in you'. And the bear hugs and kisses his mother and father and gets a good night's sleep."

Genevieve asks her daughter, "So what do you think, kiddo? Good story?"

"Good ordeal, because he passed it."

Happiness

Next morning, as Genevieve gets ready in the bathroom, the Pirate, formerly known as SJ, reads another book on her lap using only one eye.

"Momma, what is h-a-p-p-i-n-e-s-s?"

"Happiness, Miss Pirate. What's the sentence?"

"The bear went looking for happiness." SJ responds. "How do you look for happiness?" she asks.

"Happiness doesn't just come to you. If you want it you have to go find it. Just like Ralph had to find courage in order to survive the first ordeal."

"So will Ralph have to find something to get through his remaining ordeals before he finds happiness?"

"Interesting. We'll have to find out about that, won't we?"

Genevieve finishes in the bathroom, grimaces as she looks at the uncomfortable chair, then kisses and hugs the Pirate formerly known as SJ. "How you feeling?" She wants to be sure.

"Better. My stomach isn't as upset." SJ reluctantly releases her momma's hug.

"Isn't that what the doctor said, 'A little better every day'?"

SJ nods and goes back to her book, reading with her good pirate eye.

One Hundred Dollars a Week

The sun sets as Dr. Hamilton leisurely strolls through White Rock Lake Park with Michele. The shadows on the ripples on this lake offset the sparkles of dimming sunlight giving the evening a magical effect. Ducks fly overhead and skid in for a landing not too far offshore, drawing their attention. The setting sun gives urgency to their conversation, knowing the temperature will start to drop with the chill of the evening replacing the day time heat.

"I never had a bear when I was growing up." Michele seems to recollect images of her childhood in her mind's eye.

"Me neither. Guess I never knew how important something like that can be to a child, particularly one under stress like SJ."

"You impress me as a bear man." Michele shoots back with a grin.

"Not me. But I did have a plush skunk when I was three or four."

Her grin grows with this revelation, "A skunk, huh?"

"I was a strange kid, what can I tell you?"

She deliberately bumps into him and steals a kiss, which he willingly shares.

"I got us the Presidential suite at the Radisson in Santiago. That way if you want your own room…" he begins but she cuts him off with another kiss.

"Still think I want separate rooms?" she laughs at him as she pulls away.

"Guess I passed the audition."

She smiles back at him with bedroom eyes and that slightly parted set of lips which cause him to think of something other than work and SJ and bears. But he comes right back to them. He senses something important happening with SJ. Something he will want to understand, but it hasn't yet become clear to him.

"So do you know any bear stories?" he asks. Instantly he sees the parted lips draw tight. The bedroom eyes refocus.

"Just Goldilocks, I guess. Why?" her neutral response jars him.

"Her mother has to come up with the next ordeal but I'll need one after that, I expect."

"You're really getting into this, aren't you?" Her observation comes through with a certain amount of annoyance.

"It's probably like you handing an outside auditor a perfect audit trail. You want to know how you did it so you can do it again." He tries to translate it for her into something more familiar.

"Not a good comparison. What I'm concerned about is how much are you going to be obsessed with your work rather than being obsessed with me?" The tone clearly establishes that she is not convinced this will work.

"You're an independent woman. You've already got it all. I don't understand why you would want anyone obsessing about you." He tries to follow her lead, but as usual finds her way ahead of him.

She stops by a bench and sits on the top of the back rather than on the seat. This leaves her still almost at eye level with him standing. "Frankly you're a challenge, and most men aren't. I could share my bed every night with a different guy if I wanted, but you held out for eighteen months without even suggesting it. And now that we've finally consummated things, you haven't suggested it since. You even made a joke about separate rooms in Chile. If I can get you to focus on me the same way you focus on your patients I will be the most loved woman in the universe, and I know it. The trick is getting your full attention."

"I thought that's what Chile is all about; getting my full attention." He comes up behind her and puts his arms around her, nibbles at her neck and ear.

"Nibble some more, but a nanosecond in our relationship doesn't cut it. I need to know if you can leave it all behind for a week...."

He corrects her, "It's only a long weekend."

"I changed the reservations. Sounds like I should have made it for two weeks."

She breaks his embrace, stands up and looks back at him on the other side of the bench. "We've been out here for less than an hour. Every time I entice you onto something romantic or fun you instantly dive back into that little girl and her bear. If you can't leave them behind for even an hour, how are you going to do it for a week or a lifetime?"

Dr. Hamilton appraises this gorgeous woman. *She only wants me to love her as much as I love my work. This work that drives me into periodic funks - but why is that? Because I love it too much and can't bear to be less than successful every time?*

"Why do you want me totally obsessed with you? Can't there be some balance to it? I need to be able to talk about what I encounter. To have someone like you, totally objective. Who can help me see and feel the things I'm too close to." He realizes the gamble he takes may send her away. *But why have I never wanted to get too close, to expect too much. Maybe I sense she wants and needs every ounce of love I have to give. That would be the ruin of my practice.*

She reaches into an inside pocket of her coat, pulls out the tickets and extends them to him. He just looks at her, evaluating whether to pay the price of admission.

"I don't know if I can give you what you want." He admits after a moment's reflection.

"I don't think you can."

She just lets that hang in the air. She wants to see if he will take her up on it.

He still does not bite.

She continues, "But I've been a gambler all my life. If you can, then I get a love like no other. And if you can't? Well ... I'll just have to keep looking, I guess."

"No compromise," he muses aloud.

She shakes her head, "Everything in life is a compromise. I know if we are to be together there will be more compromise than either of us want. I'm a realist if that's where you're going. But I'm not willing to compromise on this. I want one true thing in my life, and that has to be our love ... total, complete and uncompromised." She again shakes her head, more to herself than to him, as if remembering something. "If I can't have that, then I don't want what's next best."

Later that evening Genevieve walks down the hallway to SJ's room totally lost in thought about all the work she left behind. She knows it will be waiting for her when she arrives in the morning. Each day she falls further and further behind. *It's not that Janie is a pain in the ass, but she asks such basic questions. How am I ever going to be able to turn my cases over to her when she just doesn't get it? Was I this slow in the beginning? I need to call Janice Ramsey. Maybe she can give me some hope that it will get better.*

She looks up. Nurses and aides are running in and out of SJ's room. She also runs… to the door. A nurse comes out and stands in her way, "No visitors at the moment."

"I'm her mother, what's the matter?" Genevieve needs to get into that room.

"I thought I recognized you." The nurse remarks. "She's having another seizure. Dr. Hamilton is on his way. We got an emergency room doctor up. She's working on her to get her stabilized."

"I need to be in there. She's gone through so much alone." Genevieve tries to push past the nurse, but the older woman won't let her pass. "She wouldn't even know you're there until it's over. And my guess is they'll sedate her when she does come out of it. She won't know you're here until the morning."

Genevieve takes a step back, "What brought this on? She seemed to be doing so much better."

"You'll have to wait for Doctor Hamilton. If you'll go down to the waiting room I'll make sure the doctor comes down after he sees her." The older nurse gently touches her and guides her in the right direction. "She has the best doctor in the hospital in my opinion. There isn't anyone like Doctor Hamilton." A worried Genevieve keeps looking back over her shoulder to SJ's room.

About three hours later Dr. Hamilton approaches the waiting room without his usual energy. Genevieve sees him first. He is still deep in thought. When she stands in anticipation, the movement catches his attention. He looks up and gives her a weaker version of his usual smile.

"You look tired." Genevieve observes, as much about herself as the doctor.

"She's stable now. Afraid she'll have to wait for Ralph the Bear's next ordeal. She's had one of her own, tonight." Genevieve instantly jumps to the undertone in his voice.

"This one was worse than before?" She asks not wanting it sugarcoated.

The doctor nods. "It lasted longer and was more difficult to bring her back." The hesitation in his voice tells her what she was afraid to hear.

"Was this a result of the treatment? Something that's part of her getting well?" Genevieve studies his body language more than the words.

"This was caused by the tumor. It apparently still grows. Even faster than we realized."

"So the treatment isn't working?" She no longer listens to the words that don't tell her what she really wants to know.

"I wouldn't say that. She's just begun. Even a cut takes time to heal."

"You said you were still looking at surgical options. What are they?" Genevieve barely recognizes her own strained voice as the fear wells up in her.

"I can't tell you with these developments. It's still getting larger. That complicates things in ways I can't predict without another MRI. I'll also need to consult with a few other specialists."

"Is she going to die?" Genevieve finally comes right out and says it. But the tremble in her voice reveals her feelings more than she would like, reveals the fear she feels overwhelming her.

"I don't know. I told you the probabilities before, forty to sixty percent recover."

The sinking feeling in her chest overwhelms Genevieve. She won't look at him but has one more question, "What do we do now?"

"I've been working with an experimental drug in clinical trials that's had positive results in cases that were not quite this far advanced. I'd recommend we try it."

"Tonight?" She finally looks into his exhausted face.

"If you sign the papers."

She picks up her clothes and bag and follows him to the nurse's station.

Genevieve lethargically walks the halls of Richland Insurance toward her cubical about two hours later than usual. Janie looks up as she walks by, but says nothing to this woman who apparently looks like death warmed over.

Dropping into her chair, Genevieve sits staring at the blank monitor for a few moments before she even turns on the switch. She waits for the password request to come up, types it in and trundles off to get some caffeine. Janie watches her pass by again.

Dean comes by, steps into Janie's cubical.

"She in yet? I see her monitor's on," He whispers so as not to attract attention of the others who are working in surrounding cubicles. Janie nods and with a head nod indicates the kitchen, mouthes the word 'coffee' without really saying it. Dean looks down the hall and sees her come out, so he walks down the hall to meet her.

Her appearance shocks him. After a brief moment, he regains his purpose, "Can you come to my office?" He asks her from about five feet away.

"Can you give me a half hour to get through the emergency call backs?"

"No, I think we need to talk now."

Genevieve rolls her eyes wondering if he would lay her off. He seems to notice and responds, "You look like hell, what's going on?"

"Is it Friday yet?" Is all she can say as she follows him to his office, "No, it's Thursday," His factual response fills her with foreboding. They step into his office and she closes the door.

"Look, I know I'm behind, I'll come in this weekend and get caught up by Monday." She intends to do it anyway.

"What's going on?"

She drops herself into the chair because she knows she will probably fall down if she doesn't sit. He continues to stand.

"I had to move out of my apartment last night. I didn't get any sleep..." A big yawn interrupts her answer. "... at all, but came right in as soon as I finished."

"What precipitated this sudden move?" Dean crosses his arms.

She looks at his body language, "Would you sit down and relax? I know I haven't told you much because it's personal, but I guess I need to tell you more than I have."

He nods and sits on his desk where he re-crosses his arms.

"I moved back into my mother's house."

"Why? If you don't think it's too personal." Dean seems annoyed and angry.

"I have hospital bills I have to pay because our insurance doesn't cover everything." She decides to appeal to something he does know about, since he has never mentioned any experience with cancer.

"Insurance never does, you should know that as well as anyone."

She realizes her fatigue overcomes her coherence as his response does not come across as what she expected. "Okay, but I'm running up a daily bill I could never have imagined. The hospital set me up on weekly payments."

This causes him to raise his eyebrow, "Weekly?"

"A hundred dollars a week. That's why I had to move back home. I couldn't cover rent and the hospital."

"You said SJ was sick, but why hospitalization?"

The tears finally let loose. She can't respond to him. He grabs tissues from a box on his credenza and brings them to her. She ignores them as the floodgates open.

A half hour later Genevieve returns to her desk, her eyes red and her face puffy. She sits down at the monitor. Just stares at it for a few moments. She reaches forward and turns the switch off, and picks up her bag. She steps over to Janie's cubical and pokes her head in. "Can you hold down the fort for a couple of days? I'll be back on Monday." Janie listens to a customer and holds up her index finger to indicate just a minute.

"I understand what you would like us to do, Mister Reynolds. I'll have to investigate the options and see what's possible. At this point this is a new problem for me and I'll have to ask a few people before I can give you a definitive answer." Janie tries to conclude the call, listens for a moment and then responds, "Yes, sir, Mister Reynolds. I understand completely. Hopefully I'll be back to you today or tomorrow at the latest. Goodbye."

"Always thank them for their business." Genevieve may be exhausted, but remembers the basics.

"Right, thanks. Are you okay?" Janie looks concerned.

"I've been better and will be, once I get some sleep. Can you hold down the fort until Monday? I'm just exhausted. Dean gave me a couple of days." Genevieve can't keep her focus on Janie.

"I'll do the best I can. Who can I go to for questions?"

"Try Helen, extension forty-eight twenty-six. Thanks," Genevieve starts to leave but Janie asks one more question.'

"Is there anything I should know?"

"About?" Genevieve seems annoyed that she would even ask.

"Guess not."

Genevieve knows she hurt Janie's feelings, but is beyond explaining anything at the moment.

Janie turns to take an incoming call, "Richland Insurance, this is Jane Peterson, how may I help you today?"

Genevieve gives her a thumbs up and slowly drags herself toward the door.

Six hours of sleep later coherence returns. Genevieve goes to see SJ at the hospital. Granma comes with her. When they enter the room SJ doesn't even seem to notice them until they are right next to her bed. She turns her head with the pirate patch still in place to look at them with her one good eye.

"Hi."

Genevieve worries at how weak SJ sounds. "You'll start feeling better soon, kiddo." Her mother leans over to give her a kiss and a hug. Granma follows the ritual.

"I did feel better, but I don't anymore. What happened, Momma?"

Genevieve sits next to her daughter. "You remember I told you that you were sick when you went to sleep at the apartment and woke up here the next morning?"

SJ nods.

"Well … what made you sick that night, made you sick again last night. But hopefully you'll feel better soon."

"I don't like being sick, Momma." SJ seems to study her mother's face for a reaction.

"We don't like you being sick either, kiddo. That's why you're here. They should be able to make you feel better quicker than if you were at home or with Granma," Genevieve decides she needs to ease into the changes.

"But I want to go home. I don't like it here."

"We talked about that, remember?" Genevieve dreads where this appears to be going.

"There's nobody to play with here."

"I know. I can play a game with you tonight." Genevieve takes her daughter's hand.

"Can you tell me the story of the bear's second ordeal instead?"

"Yes, if we can get Doctor Hamilton to come by. He wanted to hear the story too."

The Second Ordeal: The Medallion of the Cyclops

About an hour later Dr. Hamilton in his white lab coat comes in whistling, smiles at Genevieve and winks at SJ. "Looks like our pirate is ready for the next ordeal. I think this is your turn." He looks straight at Genevieve.

Genevieve tries to pick up the story where the doctor left off.

Thinks about her own situation and begins. "As I remember, Ralph the

Bear went home to get some sleep after his first ordeal."

SJ nods agreement.

"So after a good night's sleep he goes back to the Supreme Bear

Council with his parents. He watches the Master of Ordeals select

another ball from the Great Ordeals Mixer. When the Master of Ordeals

opens the ball and reads the Ordeal to Ralph --"

"Is this worse than the bridge of fire?" SJ wants to know.

Genevieve choses one of the ideas she had been considering on the

way over to the hospital. "The Master of Ordeals reads the slip of paper that says only, 'Bring back the Medallion of the Cyclops.' Every bear

gasps in horror for no bear ever returned from this dreaded ordeal."

SJ looks confused. "What's a medallion?"

"It's a piece of jewelry, in this case about six inches across. It has a

fancy face on it that the Cyclops wears around his neck on a chain."

"Do you have a medallion, Momma?"

"No, kiddo. Medallions aren't worn much anymore." Genevieve

continues, "Ralph looks to his father and says, 'I cannot do this. No bear

ever survived an encounter with the Cyclops. And Ralph's father looks

at his son and says, 'I raised you to do what is right and what is

important. You have a little girl waiting for you to prove yourself

worthy of her. I believe you are worthy for you are my son. I believe

that you will find a way to recover the medallion of the Cyclops and

come back to us.'

"Ralph turns to his mother and says, 'Mother I cannot do this. No

bear ever survived an encounter with the Cyclops. And Ralph's mother

hugs her son and says simply, 'Your father and I believe in you.'"

SJ looks to her mother and says, "So how did he find the

Cyclops?"

Genevieve continues, "The Master of Ordeals gives Ralph the directions to find the Cyclops. Ralph the Bear starts out in search of this beast that wears a medallion around his neck."

"I'll try to make this a little older for you since you didn't like the barnyard animals last time." Genevieve notes as an aside to her daughter.

"It's not that I didn't like the animals, but I'm seven. I really haven't been into animals for a while now."

Genevieve nods and returns to the ordeal. "Now Ralph has never seen any creature with only one eye. So he was curious at first, but the fear in the voice of the Master of Ordeals gave him pause. He knows he too should be afraid. But it's hard to fear something you have never seen. So Ralph takes the road before him and turns just where the Master of Ordeals said he should."

"Only one eye?" SJ seems to struggle with this idea.

"A big eye, it was. Right in the center of his face." Genevieve holds her hands in front of her own face making the shape of a large round object to help SJ see it.

The little girl pulls back in fright as Genevieve leans toward her with the one eye shaped by her hands and with a devilish grin. SJ regains her courage. She bats at her mother's hands to knock the imaginary eye away.

Genevieve drops the imaginary eye. The devilish grin that appeared with the eye is replaced with a more somber look. Genevieve looks back into her memory as she crafts the next events.

"Ralph looks about him. He soon realizes he has entered a deep and dark part of the forest that he has never been in before. But then Ralph has not been many places. So any place is probably going to be unfamiliar to him."

"Have you been many places, Granma?" SJ wonders aloud.

"Lots and lots of places, honey." Her grandmother responds.

"Like where? Have you been deep and dark in the forest?"

Granma colors into a blush, but it passes before she answers. "Many times. In fact, your great grandfather lived on the edge of the forest. When I was growing up I would wander into the deepest and darkest parts of that woods."

"Did you ever find a Cyclops or one-eyed thingy there?"

Granma feigns a search of her memory. She scratches her head and then shakes it. "Not to the best of my feeble memory. Doesn't mean it wasn't there. Just that I didn't see it. Although I remember lots of times when I thought something or someone was watching me and I couldn't see whatever or whoever it was."

SJ shudders at the thought.

Genevieve interrupts the conversation to move the story along. "Now we need to get back to Ralph, he has a long way to go here."

SJ snuggles in closer to her mother. She glances up apparently puzzled by Genevieve's smile.

"Ralph listens to the sound of the hoot owl that seems to be asking who is coming into his woods. Ralph would like to be much smaller so that it's much harder to see him; but that is not to be. Then Ralph thinks it would be good to be much bigger so he would frighten away whatever might be out there. But that is not to be either. Ralph finally abandons his thoughts of changing his size and appearance, realizing he has lost his way and no longer has any idea where he is.

"At that moment a screech owl shrieks. Ralph nearly jumps out of his fur."

SJ thinks about that for only a second, "Don't you mean skin?"

"Well bears have skin that's covered by fur. So I guess he nearly jumped out of both. But that's not the point. Ralph knows this isn't going to be easy. He doesn't have a magic sword. He doesn't have anything with him to fight a monster. And yet he feels the eyes of something upon him. Something watches him. Something that frightened the screech owl."

Genevieve accepts a bottle of water from Dr. Hamilton. She takes a sip.

"So all of his senses scan the woods around him, but it's dark. The trees and bushes are thick so he can't see. He listens. There are so many sounds of animals moving and leaves dropping off trees and the wind blowing that Ralph realizes something could be right behind him and he might not hear it. At that moment Ralph thinks he can feel hot breath upon the back of his neck. He spins around and comes face-to-face with an ugly and smelly old troll."

"What's a troll?" SJ looks to her mother for an explanation, but Dr. Hamilton answers for her.

"A troll is a magical character that lives deep in the woods, usually under bridges. The trolls are fierce fighters and protectors of their lands. They generally charge a toll to anyone who wishes to cross their lands or bridges."

"I've never seen a troll. Have you seen a troll, Granma? When you went walking in the deep dark woods?"

"I've seen drawings of trolls, but can't remember ever meeting one."

Genevieve continues. "But anyway, trolls are very nasty characters. You would know that if you ever met one. But Ralph doesn't know this about trolls, so he sneezes because the old troll smells so bad. The troll is perplexed by this behavior. He's used to the forest animals being afraid of him. He expects men to show him respect because of the long knife he wears in a sheath on his side. But no one has ever sneezed at him before. So the troll just watches Ralph as he tries to regain his composure. Each time as he thinks the sneezing is over, it starts up again. Finally the troll moves to his left so he's no longer up wind of

Ralph. Sure enough, the sneezing stops."

"Why did Ralph stop sneezing?" SJ demands of her mother.

"The wind was behind the troll so it carried the smell that was causing Ralph to sneeze. When he moved to the side, the smell wasn't so bad."

SJ nods. "That old troll must have smelled really bad."

"Trolls never bathe, so they never get clean. Can you imagine how bad you'd smell if you never had a bath?"

SJ sniffs the air in the hospital, but shakes her head, "Worse than my old socks when I play in the mud in the backyard?"

"Oh, much worse than that. Mud just smells dirty. The old troll smelled like year old sweat that has dried on you, mixed in with horse and chicken dung. And worse yet, he never washes his clothes so they trap all that smell and just make it worse."

SJ pinches her nose, "Don't think I'd want to smell that."

"Well, neither did Ralph. That was why he kept right on sneezing until the troll moved away from him. And when Ralph finally stopped sneezing, he wrinkled his nose and finally got a good look at the smelly

and ugly old troll. But Ralph is not horrified like most people would be.

In fact, he doesn't even think about the fact that the troll has warts all

over his face and a long crooked nose and green scaly skin from being

so dirty and dry all the time. No, Ralph just looks at the troll and asks.

'Who are you?'

"Now the smelly and ugly old troll is surprised to find a forest

creature who doesn't know who he is, for he is Garth, Troll King of all

the brooks in the forest. His legend lives far and wide for he protects his

lands and the creatures on them from hunters and fishermen. No one

crosses his lands without paying a toll. No one hunts or fishes here

without Garth chasing them away with his long and sharp knife. But

here is Ralph who doesn't even know who he is.

"Ralph waits and Garth the troll waits, but neither seems willing

to make the first move. This too confuses Garth the Troll King. As

royalty, he was used to others seeking to satisfy his every whim. Finally

the troll grows impatient and asks, 'I could ask the same of you, mister

bear.

"Ralph extends his paw to shake as he responds, "I'm Ralph. I must return the medallion the Cyclops wears around his neck to the Master of Ordeals."

"The smelly old troll's jaw drops at this. 'The Cyclops would never give you his medallion. That's his most prized possession. How do you plan to accomplish this task, Ralph the Bear?' And do you know what that bear said to the smelly and ugly old troll?"

SJ shakes her head.

"He said, 'I have no idea.'

"Now Garth the Troll King fought in many battles in the Troll Wars and lived to tell about it. So he made a simple observation. 'It's never a good idea to fight without a battle plan.'

"Ralph knows nothing of battles or battle plans, so he, as simply and honestly as he can, asks, "Could you help me with that?" Now, no one ever asked the smelly and ugly old troll to help them before. Everyone always ran away afraid or repulsed by him. They didn't look beyond the appearance to see that he really is a wise and kind hearted troll. The forest animals only look at his fearsome scowl and the legend of his many battles. But none ever treated him as a friend or someone who could help.

103

"The smelly and ugly old troll thought only a moment about the sons he always wanted, but never had. No troll woman would have him for a husband because of his appearance. But then again there aren't that many trolls. The forest is very large and he loved his lands so much that he never left them. That made it very hard to meet people. Maybe that was the real reason he never had even one son to raise. Anyway, the troll only thought about it for a moment and agreed to help Ralph devise a battle plan.

"The smelly and ugly old troll looked around. 'Where is your army?'

"Ralph didn't hesitate in his response, 'I have no army.'

"The smelly and ugly old troll reacted to this with astonishment. 'Then how do you propose to defeat the Cyclops in battle? I have never faced him myself. But I hear tales that he is one of the fiercest fighters in all of the forest. Almost as fearsome as myself.'

"Ralph responds simply, 'I can't defeat the Cyclops in a battle for I have no weapons and no army.'

"The troll is even more confused than before, "But that is the only way such things are done in the forest. Armies gather. Plans are made to exploit one weakness or another of the enemy. Then both sides try to kill as many of the other as possible. The winner can claim any prize from the loser he may choose. I cannot see any other way to gain the medallion from the Cyclops.'

"Ralph sits down on the ground to think. 'There must be another way. Is the Cyclops good or evil?' he asks the troll.

"The question confuses the troll. 'He must be evil for he is a Cyclops.'

"Ralph studies the trolls face. 'But you have never talked with the Cyclops. So you don't know if he is good or evil?'

"The troll doesn't even think, but blurts out his response. 'He must be evil for I have never heard anyone say a kind word about him.'

"Ralph considers, 'But would anyone say a kind word about you?'

"It's clear the troll hadn't thought of this. 'I don't know. The animals and fish that I protect, I think they appreciate what I do for them.'

"Ralph gets up and brushes the dirt off his fur. 'Have you ever asked them?'

"The troll's voice drops in realization. 'No. they run off when I appear. I think they too are afraid of me.'

"Ralph takes a step closer to the smelly and ugly old troll, but cannot take his arm as he would like as he is driven back by the overwhelming smell. 'Come with me and together we will take measure of this Cyclops. We will both learn if he is good or evil. If he is good I will reason with him. If he is evil you can engage him in combat and defeat him.'

"Now the troll had heard many stories of the Cyclops in battle. He was not eager to engage him. The Cyclops was said to be easily five times the size of the troll and many times stronger than that. But Ralph shamed him into agreeing to come along. For no King of the Trolls could admit fear. The troll did not know if Ralph realized that or what. But he could not do otherwise than agree to come."

"Did Ralph trick the troll?" SJ asks curiously.

"No. Ralph is not one to trick others, but maybe he understands troll nature."

"Is that like human nature?" Doctor Hamilton asks.

Genevieve smiles like the Cheshire cat as SJ looks back and forth between them. Genevieve then goes on with her story. "Ralph asks, 'Do you know where to find the Cyclops mister troll?'

"Garth, the King of the Trolls cannot admit that he doesn't know something, so he blusters, 'Of course I know where the Cyclops lives, but he may not be there. After all it is summer vacation time and he may have gone to the beach.'

"Ralph scratches his head. 'I did not know that a Cyclops would go to the beach on vacation. What else do you know about the Cyclops?'"

"The troll is afraid to admit that he did not even know that for sure. It was pure speculation as he really knew nothing about the Cyclops, other than the legends. 'The Cyclops is as tall as the trees. It eats a whole cow or a man or a bear at one meal. It prefers meat, but will eat fish if it is prepared with a Veronique sauce and a nice ice cold Sauvignon Blanc.' Now Ralph knows nothing of wines so he is not able to comment on the food pairings. Ralph didn't want to embarrass the troll by asking him a question and he says nothing.

"The troll was quiet for a long moment and began to drool,

apparently thinking about that meal. But then he returns to the description. 'Anyway, a Cyclops is a very dangerous creature. He only has one eye, but it bulges from his head and allows him to see things that are to either side of him. Just because he only has one eye, you cannot assume he will not notice you. The Cyclops also has a keen sense of smell. He will know you are coming miles away. And because he knows you are coming, he sends out the Bat Legions to locate you and try to drive you away before you ever reach his dark and mysterious lair.'"

"What's a Bat Legion?" SJ sounds confused.

"A Bat Legion is a flock of Bats. There are thousands of them in the flock. They all fly in formation and attack like schooled dive bombers. That's why they call them Bat Legions."

SJ frowns, apparently not completely comprehending the image her mother would have her form. Genevieve keeps on with the story.

"The troll sees that Ralph is unfazed by the thought of dive bombing bats and a dark and mysterious lair. He continues the story. 'If you get through the Bat Legions, as you approach the opening to the Cyclops' lair you must climb over a mountain of skulls and bones from the many who have attempted to reach him. The first skulls you find as you approach are of the bears. You see bears aren't particularly fearsome to a Cyclops, so he generally lets his Pretentious Guard slaughter them with arrows that rain down from the sky in the night. The bears can't see them or hear them coming in. The legends say that no bear has ever gotten past the Pretentious Guard.'

"Again, the troll can't understand why Ralph doesn't react to this horrible fate that awaits him. 'What do you think about all this, mister bear?'

"As calmly as can be, Ralph responds to the troll, 'I am sure that you will help me find a way to avoid the Bat Legions and the silent but deadly arrows from the Pretentious Guard. After all, is that not your specialty?'

"The troll now realizes that he is expected to demonstrate his bravery. He decides that nothing is going to deter this bear from his goal. 'Can you lead me there now, mister troll?' Ralph is ready.

"The troll accepts his situation. He leads Ralph back to his bridge and into the cave underneath that he fashioned over the years. In the cave are walls of shields, swords, sharp pikes and maces with which to fight. Also Ralph finds jars of nuts and dried fruits, grains and loaves of bread. The troll even has cheeses that he apparently hand made. 'You're a vegetarian!' Ralph exclaimed in sudden understanding.

"The troll looks embarrassed. 'It's much healthier you know. I wouldn't have lived to be three hundred and eighty-one if I'd been a red meat eater.'

"Ralph nods but has to ask, 'Then you're not really blood-thirsty.'

"The troll looks shocked, 'Heavens no. I'm no vampire.'"

"What's a vampire?" SJ interrupts.

"Legend has it that vampires were people who died, but were able to come back to life if they drank the blood of living things." Dr. Hamilton chimes in.

"Why would they do that?" SJ is repulsed.

"It's just a legend, can we keep moving on?" Granma seems to want to finish this story.

SJ nods but with a skeptical look.

Genevieve continues. "So. The troll takes all the shields and swords and pikes that he can carry. He leads Ralph out of his cave under the bridge and up onto the road. Up there he looks in both directions before deciding. He walks off toward the setting sun with Ralph happily following.

"They walk through the night with the troll watching the skies for the Bat Legions; but none appear. As the sun rises behind them, the troll watches the skies for the first hints of the arrows from the Pretentious Guard. No arrows appear in the sky. So they walk the whole next day with Ralph wishing he could stop for a salmon dinner as his tummy is getting hungry. It has been a long time since he last ate. Tummies wait for no bear. Ralph listens for a familiar sound, one the troll seldom pays attention to. But sure enough, Ralph hears it. He wanders into the woods to his left. The troll catches sight of the bear and stops to wait for him. Within a few minutes, Ralph follows the buzz of a bee to a hollow tree. Ralph reaches in and pulls his paw back out covered with honey and a few very upset bees.

"Ralph licks the honey from his paw as he rejoins the troll on the road. Of course the bees follow him out of the woods. In a moment the troll swings his shields to ward off the attack of the honey bees. But the bees have little trouble getting through and stinging the troll. Garth races down the road swatting at bees and occasionally dropping another sharp pike. Ralph just sits in the road, licks the honey as the bees buzz angrily about his head. His thick fur protects him from their stings.

"When he finishes, Ralph rises, brushes off the road dust and follows the road in the direction the troll and the stinging bees went.

"After sunset Ralph finds a pile of swords, shields, sharp pikes and maces next to a pond. He doesn't see the troll. After a minute Garth's head rises up in the pond.

The troll listens and looks around. 'Are they gone?'

"Ralph surveys the area and responds, 'I think so.'

"Cautiously the troll steps out of the pond and picks up his collection of weapons. 'I hope you enjoyed your snack. I'm stung from head to toe.'

"Ralph looks at the mud covered troll. 'You went to the right place. The mud is the best thing you can do for a bee sting. It pulls out the poison as it dries. You'll be right as rain in the morning.'

"The troll learns something quite by accident but is glad that he

112

will soon feel better than he does at the moment. Since the troll rested in the pond waiting for Ralph to catch up, he is ready to keep walking through the night. Ralph, on the other hand, is tired from his long walk. He decides he needs to find the Cyclops before the troll gives up the quest and returns home.

"About midnight Garth stops walking and motions for Ralph to be quiet. He hands Ralph a shield and takes one for himself. 'Quickly … get under this.' The two drop to the ground, hold the shields above them. The Bat Legions fall from the sky in a thunderous hail storm, bouncing off the shields, picking themselves back up and winging away as if dazed from the impact on those hard shields.

"The storm continues for what seems hours. Then, just as suddenly as it began, the waves of bats end and all is silent. After a few minutes the troll is the first to peek out from under his shield. He scans the sky, listening and watching, but finally trusts that the storm is over. He crawls out looking at the sea of stunned bats covering the ground for as far as the eye can see. 'It's over mister bear.'

"Ralph also crawls out from under the shield. He likewise surveys his surroundings. The troll picks up his weapons, including the shield that protected Ralph. 'We need to get away from here before they recover.' The troll advises and leads the way, stepping gingerly around the bats.

"Just before dawn Ralph and Garth arrive at the mountain of bones. Just as the troll foretold, the skulls are those of bears. Beyond them lay all kinds of animals. They begin to climb over the mountain of bones when the first arrows begin to rain down behind them. They quickly scramble through the bones, watching the arrows fall further and further behind.

"Soon Ralph and Garth come to the mouth of a huge cavern. The opening must be at least twenty-five feet tall. Bones are strewn into it. The troll looks at Ralph who shrugs. Ralph leads the way into the cavern with the troll racing past so the bear is not ahead of him.

"The cavern is dark, but candles light the way at intervals. Side passages go off into darkness. They follow the candle-lit path. The bones become further and further apart. Soon no bones can be found along the path. Then they hear sounds ahead, unlike any sounds either has heard before. It sounds like an irregular motor turning first in one direction and then in the other.

THE FIRST BEARMAS

"Suddenly they enter a huge chamber with a one hundred inch LED screen television, a massive four poster bed with canopy, a tall wine cellar next to a tapped beer keg and a barbeque pit. In the bed is a massive figure with its back to the room. The troll quietly puts down all of his weapons save a single sword. Together they silently creep up to the bed. They find a chain around the neck of the sleeping giant.

"Since Ralph doesn't have fingers, he motions to the troll to undo the chain clasp, which he does. The troll reaches forward and finds the medallion, pulls the chain from under the Cyclops' neck and steps back handing the prize to Ralph. They tip toe back to the pile of weapons. The troll has only just picked up his shield when the Cyclops stirs, rolls over revealing his singular eye, which suddenly is wide open staring at them both.

"The Cyclops roars. 'What are you doing in my lair?'

"Ralph, always the brave one, holds up the medallion and responds. 'I have come for the medallion. The Master of Ordeals charged me with returning with it so that I may prove I am worthy of a boy or girl. With my friend the troll, we have overcome all of your obstacles. We have succeeded in removing it from you while you slept.

We are leaving now and expect you to give us safe passage.'

"The Cyclops sits up in his bed, rubs the sleep from his face and looks closer at Ralph. The bear holds the medallion aloft so the Cyclops can see it better. The Cyclops rises to his full and fearsome height. He lets out an earth shaking bellow. Then he looks at the troll. 'You are the one they call Garth, are you not?'

"The troll has soiled himself, although with his hygiene problems, no one notices. 'Yes. I am Garth, King of the Trolls. Protector of the brooks and the woods and the lakes. Every living thing in the forest fears me.'

"The Cyclops nods. 'I have heard the legends from the troll wars. You are a brave troll.'

"Neither the troll nor Ralph can tell what the Cyclops thinks at that moment. The troll sheathes his sword and picks up a pike. Ralph steps back and holds the medallion close.

"The Cyclops begins to smile. 'You prepare for battle even though you cannot win. The bear refers to you as a friend. But I have never heard anyone refer to a troll as a friend. Indeed there must be magic. You survived the Bat Legions and the Pretentious Guard and removed my most precious possession without even waking me.'

"The Cyclops holds up his hand, the medallion leaps from Ralph and flies across the room to the tall beast. The Cyclops kisses the medallion and tosses it back to Ralph who catches it with both paws. 'As you wish, you may leave my lair, never to return. I give you the medallion to present to the Master of Ordeals. You have demonstrated that you are indeed worthy of a little boy or girl. But you must always remember that ordeals are shared experiences. One can only survive them when you work together, building on each other's strengths.'

"The troll quickly gathers his weapons and runs for the door. Ralph remains behind for a moment longer. 'You are indeed a wise and gracious Cyclops. While you only have one eye with which to gaze upon the world, you see the very heart and nature of things.'

"The Cyclops responded to Ralph, 'That is the curse of being a Cyclops. I must look longer and harder to see what you can with your two eyes. I must solve puzzles with less information than you. I must see what you do not by listening and hearing what is not said. You would be wise to learn to do the same."

"The Cyclops sits down on his bed as Ralph, carrying the

medallion, follows the troll back to the mouth of the cavern. "I don't know how you did that, but we are fortunate to escape with our lives.' The troll exclaims amazed.

"Ralph gives his friend a knowing smile. Together they make their way back through the woods to the troll's bridge. There they part company. Ralph gives the troll the chain that held the medallion around the Cyclops' neck. The troll gives Ralph a short sword in a sheath with a belt that he wears around his waist.

"Before returning to the road home, Ralph turns to the troll. 'Be safe my friend, for truly you are my friend. Without your help I would not have demonstrated my worthiness. You are the reason I will someday make a little boy or girl happy again. Thank you.' Ralph gives his friend a bear hug. The troll has never experienced such a sign of affection. He is speechless.

"Ralph waves from the trail and notices a tear streak the troll's face. When he arrives home Ralph sleeps soundly knowing he survived two ordeals." Genevieve looks at SJ. "Not many questions tonight. Did you like the story?"

"It's an ordeal, not a story." SJ reminds her mother, but with less energy than before.

Dr. Hamilton offers, "I guess you liked it because the bear was successful in his second ordeal?"

"And he will get his own little girl soon." The weak response reveals SJ's strength continues to erode. Both Genevieve and Dr. Hamilton notice this and exchange a look of concern. Granma doesn't seem to notice, but also didn't seem to care much for the story.

"What did you think of the ordeal, Granma?"

"I'll have to tell you the ordeal I heard at some point. If you think this was a tough one you haven't heard anything yet." Genevieve reacts to the almost challenging tone she hears in her mother's voice.

Dr. Hamilton seems intrigued as well, "Please invite me, this was great and I'm learning so much about bears."

SJ pipes up, "Me too."

The next day when Dr. Hamilton arrives to see SJ, Genevieve has gone home. SJ appears to be sleeping, but when Dr. Hamilton gets close he finds her staring off into space.

"Good morning, Miss Pirate, formerly known as SJ," he hopes she likes the running joke, but even this doesn't get a response from her. He sees her breathing but she has detached from reality. He claps his hands just once, fairly close to her. He sees SJ start and then slowly come back. In a moment she begins to move. Then her head turns toward him and she looks puzzled.

"Where were you?" The doctor asks once she engages him.

"Was I asleep? I don't know." Her puzzlement turns to confusion.

"How do you feel this morning?" His question somewhat detached as he inspects her skin color, which appears lighter than the day before.

"Where's Momma?" She looks around anxiously.

"The nurse said she went home to get some sleep in a real bed. You have to admit that chair can't be very comfortable."

SJ looks over at the chair and nods her head.

"Feel better today?" Dr. Hamilton wants her self-appraisal and so far she hasn't given him one.

"Still weak." The response validates his observation.

"And your stomach?"

"Not hungry."

Dr. Hamilton thinks back, "You need to eat something, how about some Jell-O to start and maybe some toast?" He watches as she indicates indifference with a shrug. "When was the last time you ate?"

"I don't remember." She takes a long intense look into his face. "You need to grow up"

"Excuse me?" Dr. Hamilton was thinking about her possibly losing weight when she asked her question.

"You're waiting for something."

"I am, for you to get better and go home." He responds as positively as he can knowing he fears she will not get better or go home.

"That's not what I mean."

Her comment puzzles Dr. Hamilton, "What do you mean, then?"

"Granma tells me I need to grow up," she starts off, but she does not continue immediately. Dr. Hamilton waits for her. "She says I don't know what I want."

"Is that because you want everything?" Dr. Hamilton starts to understand.

"No, I just want happiness."

"That's a pretty abstract concept for a seven year old," Dr. Hamilton observes.

"I read about it in one of my bear books. Momma explained it to me."

"So if you were to find happiness you wouldn't want anything else?" Dr. Hamilton decides to test her understanding of the concept.

"I don't know, I guess I'd still want to go to school and play with other kids."

"But would that be part of what brings you happiness?"

"I don't know."

Her thoughtful reply seems too mature for her age. He suspects she doesn't really understand. In fact, Dr. Hamilton thinks he may be reading too much into how it sounds. "So why do you think I need to grow up?"

She looks right into his eyes with her one pirate eye and studies him for a moment, then responds, "Because you don't know what you want."

"Maybe I just want others to be happy," he responds, "Maybe that's why I'm a doctor. When you're healthy and happy I can be happy."

SJ shakes her head, "But you aren't happy."

"Oh, I think I'm as happy as the next person." His response just comes out without much thought. Even he surprises himself with the flippancy of it.

"You're not as happy as the nurse."

Her observation surprises the doctor. "Well … she's just a happy person."

"Why is she happier than you?"

Dr. Hamilton wonders if SJ is simply repeating a conversation she had with her mother. It just doesn't make sense otherwise. But he realizes SJ is waiting for an answer to her last question about the nurse. "She doesn't have the responsibilities I have as a doctor."

"Maybe you should be a nurse. Then you could be happy too." SJ rolls over facing away from Dr. Hamilton. This has been an unsettling conversation for him and he wonders *why is she concerned about happiness?*

Dr. Hamilton tries to connect dots, "Is your Momma happy?"

SJ doesn't move, but responds, "No."

"She's happy she has you as her daughter. She clearly loves you very much." Unsure where to take this he makes a guess. "Is everything hard for you and your mother?"

"Yes."

"Are you part of all those hard things?" He continues trying to put it together.

"I'm sick."

"But everyone gets sick from time-to-time." He doesn't want her to think of herself as a burden to her mother.

"Not hospital sick."

"No, most people don't come to the hospital very often, but they do when they need to. Right now, you need to be here until we fix you up. That's why hospitals exist."

"But I want to go home."

"You will soon." He tries to comfort her.

"I can't ever go home." She sounds very disappointed and begins to cry.

"Sure you will."

"Momma moved. I can't go home." SJ seems very upset, almost angry. He guesses she feels helpless her mother moved and she can't do anything about it.

"Why did your Momma move?" Dr. Hamilton asks, but then doesn't follow up probably realizing it isn't any of his business.

"I can't go home," SJ continues to cry.

That afternoon Genevieve walks down the hall towards SJ's room. The energy has returned to her determined step. She looks much more rested. As she passes the nurse's station she says 'hello', but the nurse stops her. The nurse asks Genevieve to go to Dr. Hamilton's office when she has a chance. Nothing immediate, but he would like a chance to talk with her, not in front of SJ. Genevieve has a sense of foreboding and decides to put it off until later.

SJ naps when Genevieve enters her room, so she puts her things down and decides maybe this may be the best time to find the doctor. She walks across the square between buildings, looking at the trees that have lost their leaves. She thinks the weather reflects her mood of foreboding. The low hanging clouds threaten rain. She enters the marble and granite medical office building and finds his suite. The receptionist asks her to wait and he will see her when he finishes with a patient. He can do this now because his next patient called and will be arriving late. Genevieve picks up a magazine and just gets into an article about travel to Chile when the nurse calls her name. They walk back to Dr. Hamilton's office. She still has the magazine and continues reading the article. A knock on the door precedes Dr. Hamilton entering and sliding in behind his messy desk.

Genevieve closes the magazine, but keeps it on her lap.

"There's a good article on Chile in that one." He starts the conversation.

"I was just reading it. Never been, have you?" She gratefully wants to talk about something else.

"No, but I plan to soon."

She nods thinking a doctor can go to Chile, but an insurance claims assistant never will. "You wanted to see me about something."

"I had a conversation with SJ this morning. I want to better understand it."

Genevieve relaxes realizes it isn't more bad news, but his tone perplexes her, "Sure. What did she say?"

"Have you and SJ had any conversations about me?" He seems rather defensive.

"Just that she likes you very much and thinks you tell great ordeals." Genevieve realizes that probably reflects her feelings more than SJ's, so she adds, "But we really haven't talked about you... very much."

Dr. Hamilton doesn't appear satisfied by her answer, so she continues, "Did she say I said something?"

"No, no. She said she thought I needed to grow up."

"She said what?" This amazes Genevieve.

"Why do you think a seven year old would make a comment like that?"

Genevieve listens to his question and the tone seems to be more curious than angry, which she thought he might be.

"That's totally beyond me. What was the context?"

"Happiness. Were you talking about happiness?" Dr. Hamilton looks puzzled and his usual ready smile has gone AWOL.

"Well ... yes, it was in one of her books. We talked about it." Genevieve tries to understand why SJ would be talking about happiness.

More to himself than to her he says, "That tracks." But then he looks up at Genevieve and asks, "Do you think I'm happy?"

Genevieve flounders for a moment before collecting her wits. "Did she say she didn't think you were happy? Is that what this conversation is all about?"

"She did say that, but I'm asking your opinion."

"Well ... you seem happy, relatively speaking ... I guess."

"You hedged that well. Do you know what she said? She said the nurse was happy and maybe I should be a nurse so I could be happy too."

"She didn't." Genevieve is totally embarrassed.

Dr. Hamilton nods with a stifled smile, which finally breaks through to a genuine smile he shares with Genevieve. "You have a remarkable daughter."

"That's certainly one word you could use." But Genevieve thinks of another.

"I take it there are others you'd prefer not to share?" Dr. Hamilton observes.

"Maybe when I get to know you better."

I didn't just say that, did I?

"Okay. I feel better. Do you often have such adult conversations with your daughter?"

Genevieve rolls her eyes, "Guilty as charged."

"Why is that?" Dr. Hamilton asks gently.

"I want her to make something of herself, to be a free thinker, to really understand the world and be able to change it through sheer determination and will power." Genevieve could go on and on, but cuts herself short, not wanting to embarrass herself.

"That's quite ambitious. Do you think most parents have such bold plans for their children, especially at such a young age?"

"As I reflect on what my parents wanted, I think their expectations diminished as I got older and they could see what I was really capable of being … what I actually did make of myself." She speaks softer and almost with sadness as she adds the last few words.

"Do you think you disappointed your parents?" He reacts to her conclusion.

Genevieve tears up, looks away and simply nods once.

The Third Ordeal: Ending the Fairy Wars

SJ waits impatiently for Dr. Hamilton to arrive. It's time for another ordeal. Dr. Hamilton promised he would stop by this evening. It is now much later than anyone expected. She knows that her mother will want her to go to sleep soon. The nurses poke their heads in periodically looking to see if the doctor has arrived. The ordeals have become the talk of the hospital. It's clear to SJ that the nurses want to hear the stories the doctor tells her as much as she does.

Genevieve seems distracted too, as if she were hoping to see the doctor. She keeps fussing with her hair and wrapping a lock behind her ear. When her mother does that SJ knows she's nervous about something. That's one of those things that only appear under certain circumstances. SJ realizes her mother probably doesn't know she does it.

Then she hears his voice in the hall. A smile appears on her mother's face. SJ wonders why this doctor seems to make her mother feel better when he hasn't done a very good job of making her feel

better. *Another mystery to solve before I go back to school. Even if the kids are*

different at this new school. New friends to make, she can hear her

Granma say.

Dr. Hamilton comes in. Several of the nurses follow him. One

pushes a frail looking boy a little older than SJ. Jacob is in the hospital

for the same treatment. Only he has been here longer than SJ. The

nurses and Jacob line up along the wall to listen. Dr. Hamilton turns to

look at them. "What's this?"

The older charge nurse looks at the others and simply responds,

"We heard this was the best entertainment in the hospital. Just wanted

to get in on a good thing."

Dr. Hamilton shrugs and takes a look at SJ. "So you ready for

another ordeal?"

SJ nods and looks at Genevieve, who smiles self-consciously but

avoids eye contact with the doctor. He seems to notice this, but sits

down at the foot of SJ's bed. The doctor looks around as if trying to

remember something and then begins with a smile.

"So, Ralph rested for a week before he was able to return to the

Supreme Bear Council with his parents. He watches the Master of
Ordeals select another ball from the Great Ordeals Mixer.

"When the Master of Ordeals opens the ball and reads the Ordeal
to Ralph –"

"I can't imagine what would be worse than the Cyclops." SJ
remarks to her mother.

"The Master of Ordeals reads the slip of paper that says only, 'End
the Fairy Wars.' Every bear gasps in horror, for no bear ever ended a
war, let alone one amongst the fairies.

SJ gazes off into the distance with a perplexed look as if trying to
picture fairies at war in her mind's eye.

"Well anyway," Dr. Hamilton continues, "Ralph looks to his father
and says, 'I cannot do this. No bear ever stopped a war by himself. And
Ralph's father looks at his son and says, 'I raised you to do what is right
and what is important. You have a little girl that waits for you to prove
yourself worthy of her. I believe you will find a way to end this needless
war and come back to us.'

"Ralph turns to his mother and says, 'Mother I cannot do this. No bear ever ended a war. And Ralph's mother hugs her son and says simply, 'Your father and I believe in you.'"

SJ looks to her mother and says, "Why are the fairies fighting?"

Her mother nods to the doctor to listen.

Dr. Hamilton continues, "So the Master of Ordeals gives Ralph the directions to find the fairies."

"As Ralph leaves the Hall of the Supreme Bear Council he remembers the many stories his mother told him as a young bear. The stories often recounted the exploits of wizards and goblins, witches and werewolves, but she seldom told him of the fairies. He realizes that he really doesn't know much more about fairies than that Tatania was a good fairy and that she loved Peter Pan. He knows this will not help him in his current quest. He never thought about fairies raising armies. He thought they were friendly types and always willing to help a lost soul in the woods or perform some magical feat. The thought of a fairy war was just simply beyond his comprehension. How do fairies fight? Do they cast spells? Do they sprinkle fairy dust and just watch their opponents float off into space? As Ralph thinks about it, he isn't even sure they have wings and can fly. Although Tatania did. Since that is his only reference point, he thinks that probably is the case."

SJ gains a cross expression. "Of course fairies can fly. Doesn't Ralph know anything?"

Dr. Hamilton gauges SJ's anger. He decides to adjust his story. "Of course Ralph knows many things. Do you know how to catch a salmon in a stream with your 'bear' hands?

SJ's anger lessens and she defensively responds, "Not with my 'bear' hands cause bears don't have hands."

"That's right, they have paws, don't they?"

SJ nods as if confirming she is smart after all.

"So Ralph knows many things, he just doesn't know much about fairies. At this point he wishes his mother had told him more stories about them. Then, he would have a better idea of what to expect on this ordeal. But Ralph remembers what his father always said in such instances, 'It is what it is.' Ralph thinks about that for a moment. He tries to decide if there is anything he can do to learn more about fairies before he finds himself in the middle of their war. But think as much as he can, he doesn't come up with any ideas."

"He should ask me. I know all about fairies." SJ pronounces

proudly.

"I didn't know that." Dr. Hamilton observes. "Tell me about their armies and how they fight."

SJ looks less sure, glances as her mother who shrugs and then contritely responds to the young doctor. "My fairies don't fight. They're good fairies."

"Do you think all the people in the Army are bad people because they fight?"

SJ looks to her mother to save her from this line of questioning.

Genevieve sees her daughter's plight and responds, "Of course not. People go into the Army to protect their country. They're good people doing their patriotic duty."

Dr. Hamilton nods. "It's the same for the fairies. They're good. But when they're threatened, they come together to protect each other. They don't want to fight. They don't want to hurt anyone or anything. But sometimes they find themselves in a situation where they must protect themselves. They got into this war because one group of fairies wanted something another group of fairies had."

"What did the fairies want?" SJ demands to know.

"Fairy dust. You see, one year there was a shortage of fairy dust. Since all the fairies need it to fly, those who didn't have enough decided to start a war to take it from another group of fairies."

"So what happened to Ralph?" SJ reminds him.

"Ralph? Well as I remember, we left our hero, Ralph the Bear, wandering into the forest one more time, wondering why he really doesn't know much about fairies.

"And I said I know all about them."

"That's right. So, Ralph listens to the creepy forest wind blowing through the trees. He listens to the rustling of leaves that mask the movements of the many forest creatures. Now Ralph knows something, and more likely, many creatures are watching him in his quest to find fairies. He would like to stop and ask the unseen creatures where he should look to find the fairies. But since the creatures continue to remain out of sight, he does not. Instead, he continues walking, humming softly and watching the forest get denser and darker."

"But Ralph's been in the forest his whole life. He should be used to it by now." SJ is anxious to find the fairies.

"Are you used to the first few minutes after the lights go out in your bedroom at night?" Dr. Hamilton responds.

"It's scary until I go to sleep." SJ admits.

"It's the same for Ralph. No matter how many times he enters the forest, it's always scary until he gets used to it. Even then, he carefully listens and watches and is always on his guard for the unexpected."

SJ shudders in response to the doctor's description. He notes this and moves on.

"So, Ralph wanders deep into the forest. Since he doesn't know where he will find the fairies he decides it doesn't make any difference where he wanders to. He follows the path before him. Ralph really doesn't mark the path or do anything that will help him find his way out. He doesn't have a plan for how he will return, as he realizes he will probably do so by a very different trail than the one he takes today."

"Can I have my juice?" SJ points and Genevieve retrieves it for her. The doctor waits for her to finish before he continues.

"So, Ralph comes to a beautiful pool of water deep in the heart of the dark and creepy forest. A brook runs into it. The sound of gently running water fills the air. Ralph senses this is a magical spot. He hopes a fairy or two might appear. He leans over the still waters to take a drink. When he raises his head from the water he sees a reflection of someone behind him. Quick as a flash, Ralph rises up and spins around to find that he is face-to-face with... his friend, Garth the King of the Trolls. 'Garth! What are you doing here in the deepest and darkest part of the forest?'

"Garth responds with surprise and an anxiousness that Ralph doesn't remember. 'Ralph. Which side are you on?'

"Ralph doesn't understand the question. He glances around and guesses. 'Your Southside?'

"The troll rapidly scans the area as he answers. 'Wrong question. Whose side are you on?'

"Ralph doesn't hesitate. 'Why yours of course.'

"Garth hears something and brings his shield higher. 'Then you're with Tatania and the Fairyland Raiders. You chose the right side. I'm pleased to see you wearing the sword I gave you. It will serve you well in the coming battle.'

"Ralph checks the sword on his belt, realizes he never removed it from the sheath. He pulls it out part-way to be sure it's all there. Then looks up at his friend. 'What's going on here?'

"The troll hears something and signals for Ralph to be quiet. In a moment a beautiful tiny fairy floats in on rapidly beating wings. She stops just a few inches from Garth's face. 'Thunderclap divided his troops. He's trying to attack on both flanks simultaneously. It leaves a weak middle. I know we can break through, but we have to leave skirmish troops back to alert us where and when they're coming from behind.'

"Garth shakes his head. 'Better to attack the flanking forces than to go head on with those who are dug in and have established defenses, Tatania. Create a small diversionary attack on one end of their line. Have your main forces seize the initiative and destroy those troops attempting to flank. They will have few defenses up and will not be expecting you.'

"Ralph listens to this discussion and blurts out, 'You make this sound like a game, but it's not. Fairies will die.'

"Both the words and the emotion of hatred underlying Tatania's response surprises Ralph. 'Good. More fairy dust for us.'

"Ralph shakes his head. 'You can't mean that. You can always find more fairy dust, but you can never replace a fallen fairy.'

"Garth provides a measured response to Ralph. 'You don't understand, my friend. Without fairy dust the fairies have to walk everywhere. They can't fly up into the flowers where they gather the pollen and nectars that are their food. They can't perform the magic that comforts the creatures of the forest.'

'Without fairy dust it would be the end of civilization as we know it.' Tatania adds.

"Ralph sits down to think. In only a moment the answer comes to him. 'But there is plenty of fairy dust. It's just that you have not learned to conserve and share it until the shortage is over.'

"Tatania responds quickly. "The shortage will never be over. There is only just so much fairy dust. When it's gone, it's gone.'

"Still seated, Ralph thinks again for a moment and then responds. 'But there must be alternatives to fairy dust. Maybe you can make alternative fairy dust from reprocessed plant nectar or reconstituted

Queen Anne's lace.'

"Tatania's fairy dust is running low so she lands on Garth's shoulder before she loses too much altitude. She looks at Garth as she asks, 'Is he your friend? He certainly has a lot to learn,' Tatania looks directly at Ralph. 'Fairy dust alternatives are just another fairy tale. They cost too much and take too long to make. They also haven't figured out how to make enough to have an impact. Any fairy who expects to continue doing their job and intends to rely upon alternatives is smoking something.'

"Ralph thinks some more. 'Have you done your job since the war began?'

"Tatania's eyes narrow. 'What do you mean?'

"Ralph leans his head to the left to strike a thoughtful pose. 'I assume you are using all of your fairy dust to fight the war. With the shortage you must be rationing it. That would not leave any to do normal fairy things.'

Tatania sounds angry. 'What are you trying to say, bear?'

"Ralph rises and dusts himself off. 'That the war is consuming all your resources. And all that you will need for the future. In a war, no one wins. You are mortgaging the future of your children. How long before you save up enough fairy dust to return to your former life? Never. You have changed your society. Now there will be fairies who have fairy dust and fairies that do not. Isn't it better for all fairies to learn to do with less and still enjoy normalcy within limits?'

"Tatania shakes her head. 'No. The Fairyland Raiders will not have to live with limits. It takes away our freedom. We should be able to live the idyllic lives we have always lived.'

"Ralph continues to brush off the road dirt, does not look at Tatania. 'But the world has fundamentally changed, Tatania. We no longer live in an age of limitless existence. We must find ways to live together in peace and harmony and share the resources. Only when everyone can enjoy the same benefits of living in our world will we all find the idyllic existence you remember, but no longer enjoy. You are too busy trying to regain that which you have already lost.'

"Tatania looks at Garth. 'Is he one of those new age guys? I thought they were just fairies and were all killed at the battle of Fairyland Sea.'

"Garth looks sadly at Ralph. 'It must be a disease, Tatania. Looks like it jumped species. Guess we will have to quarantine him to make sure it doesn't infect the troops.'

"Tatania shakes her head. "I say we just kill him. That way it can't spread."

SJ cries out, "No. You can't kill Ralph. He's a good bear."

Dr. Hamilton smiles at SJ before he continues. "Yes, he is a good bear, but let's see what happens, shall we?"

SJ nods, but her eyes are red and moist. She hugs Genevieve fearful for the outcome.

"Ralph doesn't answer Tatania. He has a heavy heart that reason and logic seems to have no effect on the fairy warlord. Even Garth doesn't seem willing to come to the aid of his friend. But just then, Tatania opens the sack of fairy dust that she carries attached to her sash. She reaches inside. 'Oh, no. I'm out.' She exclaims. 'I'll have to wait and hope the others have enough for me.' Garth looks surprised, but quickly hides it. Ralph stands waiting for other fairies to arrive. But they wait a long time. Nothing happens. The sun goes down. And no fairies arrive to help Tatania.

"Ralph gets tired of waiting so he suggests to the others, 'Why don't I gather some wood. We can have a nice fire and some dinner.'

"Tatania observes, 'Fine for you, but I don't eat what you do.'

"Ralph winks at Garth, 'Not a problem, Tatania. If Garth will carry you over to those beautiful flowers you can feast on the abundance of nectar. I'll build a fire to keep us warm. Then I'll gather nuts and honey for Garth and myself. If we work together we can all rest comfortably for the night and wait for your troops to come and kill me tomorrow.' And that is what they did. Ralph built a small fire with kindling. He gathered nuts and berries and brought them back to the fire to share with Garth. Then he went further into the woods and found a honey tree. He dipped his paw in and carried his honey covered paw back to the fire as well. There, he and Garth licked the rich dark honey all off. When they finished, Ralph washed his paw in the mirror-like pond.

"Tatania lay down, not too close to the fire, but close enough to stay warm as wearing a simple leotard doesn't keep her warm through the night. Garth and Ralph eat the berries and nuts and talk about their ordeal with the Cyclops. Tatania listens to their war story. When they are through she remarks, 'That's a nice story. No one dies and Ralph proves he's worthy.'

"Garth looks at Ralph as he continues the thought. 'And we worked together to do it. Neither of us could have defeated the Cyclops alone. We built upon our strengths to achieve what we both wanted.'

"Ralph let that thought be the last of the night before he curls up in front of the fire. After a long period of seeming to be, while he thought of ways to end the conflict, he finally went to sleep."

"I don't think I could sleep if someone was going to kill me in the morning." SJ reaffirms that she is following the story.

"I might have a little trouble with that myself." Genevieve chimed in as she studies the doctor, clearly curious about how this is going to end.

"Not me. Nothing keeps me from a good night's sleep." Granma informs everyone. "That's one good thing about getting older. None of this means nothing. We all know you can't have an unhappy ending so let's just cut to the chase."

The doctor continues the story. "Ralph woke up several times during the night only to find that Tatania is usually awake, watching for her troops to arrive. Garth is fast asleep, in a dreamless sleep much as trolls, who have seen much in their lives, experience. It's almost as if they do not allow themselves to dream about what they have seen or done for fear that they will never be able to dream about anything else should they do so."

"I have the same dream a lot." SJ notes to no one in particular.

Surprised, Genevieve asks, "And what is that dear?"

"I dream of looking at something magical out my window, and when I reach for it, I fall. Only I never stop falling."

Dr. Hamilton glances up quizzically at Genevieve, who returns the look as if hoping for an interpretation. The doctor is hoping for some insight from her that he can see is not forthcoming.

"Are you frightened?" The doctor asks.

"No. It's a very slow fall, like I'm floating and not really falling at all."

"Does the fall ever end?" The doctor follows up.

"No. I wake up before it does."

143

Dr. Hamilton nods in understanding, looks at an anxious Genevieve for a moment and then resumes the story. "Ralph listens each time he awakens, hoping to hear the sound of a million fairy wings descending to carry him to his fate. But no such sound greets him. In fact, the sounds of the forest creatures seem to have blended into an uncomfortable silence. It seems to Ralph as if something were lurking in the woods. The creatures seem to wait for it to take its prey and get on with life ... and death.

"When the morning light began to illuminate the horizon Ralph stretches and stifles a yawn. He is not rested, by any means. It was a restless sleep. He knows today will not only determine his fate, but also the outcome of the fairy wars, of that he is sure.

"Tatania sits with her back to a tree, but her head rests upon her chest with her eyes closed. Garth's snoring is what probably woke Ralph, but he can't remember. He is much more interested in a rustling in the forest that he does not recognize. It is both distant and close, hushed, but unmistakable. Ralph watches for some sign of the source of this curious sound. He wonders if Tatania and Garth will awaken before it reached their location.

"And then they are there. All around them at once, marching, not quite like a military regiment, but in a distinctly organized fashion. Fairies. Hundreds, no thousands of fairies fill the clearing from all directions. Most collapse to rest. Those behind stumble on them and fall head-over-heals. It is a most remarkable sight for a bear not used to the ways of the magical woods, having grown up in the humdrum ordinary woods near the towns of the people.

"And still Tatania and Garth sleep on. Ralph asks the fairy closest to him, who is now prostrate with exhaustion. 'What's happened?'

"The fairy looks up at Ralph as if it were an ordinary occurrence to talk with a bear, and answers quite clearly for a very tired fairy. 'No more dust.'

"And of course this only piques the interest of this big brown bear. 'What ever do you mean?'

"The response is quick in coming. 'Just what I said brother bear. We are completely out of fairy dust. We cannot defend ourselves. We must be ready to surrender to the heathen fairies.'

"Ralph has not head this term to describe fairies. He wants to satisfy his curiosity. 'What do you mean, heathen?'

"The fairy closest has now recovered enough to have a conversation, which, if you know fairies, is something they take great pride in having. 'Those we have been fighting. They are not true believers. They actually think fairy dust is not divinely provided and we can make our own.'

"Ralph didn't know that fairies divide into different groups. This is the first time he has ever heard about true believers. He thinks about this for a moment. Without thinking says, 'Oh. You're talking about the New Agers.'

"Almost instantaneously, as if all the fairies are one, a collective gasp fills the woods. It is enough to wake the sleeping Tatania and even cause Garth to turn over in his sleep. Tatania focuses and after a moment to gather her wits, rises and calls out to her troops. 'Friends, Fairylanders and countrymen, lend me your dust, for I have no more with which to carry on the fight.'

"With this call to arms, none of the fairies will look at Tatania. She instantly senses the mood of her troops. 'What's wrong? Why do you turn away?'

The fairy closest to Ralph seems to be a lieutenant of Tatania and stands to address her commander. 'Your brilliance. We do not have fairy dust to share.'

"Tatania waves this away. 'Surely for your commander and comrade-in-arms … you could find…' But Tatania sees that no one will return her gaze. 'What is it?'

"The lieutenant finishes her original thought. 'We do not have any fairy dust amongst us at all. We have exhausted our supplies fighting the war.'

"Garth awakens as the lieutenant finishes her report. 'Then we must build defenses to protect ourselves.' The troll rises to his feet and unsheathes his sword holding it high over his head.

"But the lieutenant shakes her head and looks directly at her commander. 'I don't think that will be necessary, your brilliance.'

"Tatania reads this situation and calls for a final validation of what she thinks is happening. 'So the heathens are out of fairy dust as well?'

"The lieutenant finally summons the courage to look Tatania in the eye. 'It will take us and them a decade to rebuild supplies to the pre-war levels. And that is only if we manage them carefully.'

"Tatania reads between the lines. 'You're talking rationing?'

"The lieutenant, completes the ugly report. 'Yes, unless we adopt the artificial production methods of the heathens. If we were to do that we could match them ounce for ounce. If we do not they will quickly surpass our production. They will be able to re-engage us in war in about five years.'

"Ralph notes, 'No war for at least five years and probably not even then if you match their production.'

"Garth exclaims, 'How awful, no war for five years.'

"And Ralph responds, 'How wonderful. No wars for at least five years. Sounds like a no-brainer to me.'

"Garth approaches Ralph. 'What are you supposed to bring back this time?'

"Ralph responds, 'A signed copy of the declaration ending the war. I'll help them draft it.'

Garth nods and goes to prepare the parchment upon which the final declaration will be signed by all parties. And knowing of Ralph's need for a copy he prepares the copy as well.

"The next day the parchment agreement to end the war is signed into law by the leaders of both groups, the New Agers and the True Believers. Ralph is presented a beautiful embroidered copy by the Deputy Commander of the Fairyland Rangers. Ralph tucks this document into the belt with the sharp sword given him by Garth, even though he has never used it. He says goodbye to the fairies, and to Tatania. The goodbye to Garth takes a little longer. Ralph presents him with a silver chalice full of nuts and berries. Garth presents him with a beautiful silver shield to match the sword previously given him. Their good-bye ends in a bear hug they will both long remember.

"As Ralph starts on the long journey home he remembers the first parting from Garth and how they learned to help each other. This time they are able to achieve even more without the need to explain what each was doing. Ralph finally understands just how important it is having a friend to support you in reaching your goals."

SJ stares off in the distance for a moment. "Why didn't the fairies talk to each other and try to find a way to help each other?"

Genevieve answers with a question, "And why don't you talk to me about how you feel rather than making me guess?"

SJ looks at her mother with her one good eye. "Because when

you're happy you make me laugh."

Genevieve shakes her head, "What does that have to do with how you feel?"

"I haven't felt good in a long time."

Genevieve sits back, realizing what her little girl tries to say to her.

"I haven't felt good in a long time, either." Jacob adds to the conversation. Everyone turns to look at the little freckle-faced boy with the white skin. SJ had met Jacob earlier when she was going to tests. SJ realizes Jacob probably feels just like she does, only he's been having to deal with it a lot longer.

"Did you like Ralph's ordeal?"

Jacob answers sadly, "My grandmother used to tell me stories."

"She doesn't anymore?" SJ asks.

Jacob shakes his head, "She died."

SJ looks up to Granma who is watching Jacob and shaking her head. Genevieve gives SJ a hug from behind, but still SJ just watches Granma.

Dr. Hamilton reviews more test results for SJ. He leans his elbows on his desk and runs his hands though his hair, trying to think of something he can do. He looks at the telephone for a long time, then checks the clock on his wall and dials a memorized number.

"Michele Franklin." The response seems like someone in the middle of something to him.

"Hey, gorgeous, you have a minute?" Dr. Hamilton asks.

"No, Stephan, I don't."

Caught by surprise, Dr. Hamilton can't say anything.

Dead silence precedes her continuing, "Uhhh. Stephan?"

"It's Jackson." His mouth all dry, he finds it difficult to get the words out. "When you have a minute can you give me a call at the office?" He hangs up.

Less than a minute later his phone rings. He looks at it for a long time before he picks it up. "Jackson? I'm sorry," Michele sounds unsure of how to proceed.

"My fault, I should have identified myself."

"Why do you instantly blame yourself for everything that happens?"

"Stephan's your boss, isn't he?"

"Yes."

Dr. Hamilton reconsiders his purpose, "I need someone to talk to, but I don't want to bother you at work."

"Talk to me Jackson."

"I'm losing her." Dr. Hamilton hardly recognizes his own voice.

"This the seven year old?" Michele guesses.

"I've put her on an experimental treatment and even that doesn't seem to slow it down. I don't know what else to do." His voice conveys his feelings of helplessness.

"Why is this one so special to you?"

"I don't know. There's just something about her." Dr. Hamilton sees the pirate patch and the mischievous smile listening entranced by the bear ordeals. Then the little girl in convulsions whose body's reactions have overcome her reason.

"What can I do to help you?"

"Nothing, this was a mistake. I shouldn't have called you."

"Jackson?"

He hangs up and leans back in his chair, unable to get his mind off of SJ and her deteriorating test results.

Genevieve approaches the door to SJ's room on Monday evening. Her first day back at work was a long hard day. She tried to get caught back up. But she had to work through the anger of customers who waited several days for her to get back to them with answers. She prides herself in always getting answers the same day. But she was exhausted and couldn't go on.

She knows that SJ's condition continues draining her both mentally and physically. At work she only gets about half as much done as she used to. While today was better than the rest, she still didn't achieve a normal day's work for her. While Dean seemed more accommodating today than previously, she knows she still doesn't perform to his satisfaction. That can't keep going on.

And then there's Janie. She seems to want to help, but not. It seems to Genevieve Janie sees this whole thing as an opportunity to establish herself. It seems she does everything she can to ingratiate herself with Dean. She heard them whispering in Janie's office more than once today. Dean never whispers and almost never talks to anyone in their office. She doesn't know what's going on there, but she suspects it will not end up in her favor when it sorts itself out.

She comes back out of her reflection on the day when she hears SJ yelling at the top of her voice, "You're hurting me. Get out! Where's my Momma?" A moment later Genevieve steps into the room and finds SJ with the pirate patch on the wrong eye, jumping up and down on the bed, pushing away two nurses, one on each side of the bed, as they try to corral her and get her to sit down.

"I'm here, SJ." Genevieve calls out as she steps into the room.

"Momma! They're hurting me. I want to go home." SJ stops bouncing on the bed and crawls off to run to her mother. She throws her arms around Genevieve and hugs her desperately.

Genevieve looks at the nurses trying to understand what upsets SJ. They pick up the untouched breakfast tray and the untouched lunch tray and carry them out. One nurse leans toward Genevieve and says, "Stop down to the nurse's station and we'll give you an update. It's been a hell of a day."

Genevieve kneels down to SJ and gives her a hug, "What's the matter, kiddo?"

"They're hurting me."

"How are they hurting you? Looked to me like they just wanted you to sit down."

SJ pinches her mother's arm, "They were pinching me and trying to hold me down in the bed."

Genevieve moves the patch to be over the right eye and the left instantly moves to look at her. "Can you see better now?"

"Yes."

"Why did you move the patch? You couldn't see anything, could you?"

"I didn't want to see them pinching me."

"Why were they pinching you?"

"I don't know, Momma."

"Why were they trying to hold you down?"

"I don't know."

Genevieve gives SJ a quick hug again, "Well I'm glad to see you bouncing again. That means you must be feeling better."

"My stomach doesn't hurt so much."

"Didn't look like you ate anything," Genevieve tries to confirm with her daughter.

"No. I'm still not hungry. Ouch." SJ slaps her mother's face.

"Why did you do that?"

"You pinched me."

"I didn't. Where do you think I pinched you?"

SJ reaches around to her right side with her left hand. "Here."

Genevieve pulls SJ's shirt up and looks at the spot. A quick examination reveals no red spots, or other indications of a pinch or any other contact. "I don't see anything. Are you sure you were pinched?"

SJ nods.

"I don't think you're being pinched, but you could be feeling something else." Genevieve offers. "Why don't you go sit down on your bed and read you bear book for a few minutes? I'll be right out here in the hall."

SJ walks over, picks up her book and then climbs up into the bed. She adjusts the pirate patch and begins to read softly to herself.

Genevieve walks out to the nurse's station and finds the nurse who spoke to her as she left SJ's room. "What's going on?"

The nurse motions for the other to join the conversation. "She was just one holy terror all day. She argued over whether she could read her book. She argued she didn't want to eat the food. She argued she should be able to go to the bathroom and not have to keep the door open. She argued she should be able to change her clothes when she wanted to. She argued we were pinching her and we needed to stop. We asked her to read quietly and she started bouncing on the bed. She'd been doing that for at least ten minutes when you arrived. Like I said, it's been one hell of a day."

"What were the pinches all about?" Genevieve demands to know.

"Best I can think is she's having tingling sensations and she's interpreting the tingles as pinches. Only thing that makes sense to me." The first nurse responds to her question.

"Have you ever seen this behavior before?" Genevieve asks.

The second nurse pipes up, "Not this bad. Kids go through mood swings sometimes, but she was just all over the place and arguing everything."

"So this is something she'll pass through. Is that what you're saying?" Genevieve studies the two nurses to be sure they agree.

"Hopefully. We'll just have to see." The first nurse finally responds. "Sounds like you had a positive effect already. That room hasn't been this quiet all day."

"Probably the vodka I put in her bottle." Genevieve jokes.

"You do that too? Just a little worked every time on my little ones." The second nurse admits and laughs.

Genevieve gets serious again. "What does this mean? Do I need to do anything?"

"She's got cells in her brain doing strange things. No telling what's going to happen next. The only one who knows what's going on ain't talking to us about it." The first nurse seems to study Genevieve as she responds.

"Doctor Hamilton?" Genevieve asks.

"Even he don't know." The second nurse responds.

"Oh." Genevieve finally realizes they aren't talking about a person.

Genevieve looks at the door to SJ's room and listens. No sounds come from it, no disagreeable rages, or screams from imaginary pinches.

The Fourth Ordeal: The Jungle

The next evening, Granma comes to visit about the time Genevieve arrives from work. They meet in the hallway and Genevieve gives her mother a quick peck on the cheek, which her mother accepts without reciprocating. As they pass the nurse's station Genevieve looks to the nurse. "How is she today?"

"Quiet." The worrisome response from the nurse gets Genevieve's attention.

"The argumentative behavior? Pinching? Anything?" Genevieve asks with as much gesture as words.

The nurse shakes her head and shrugs.

Genevieve's mother asks, "What was that all about?"

"Yesterday wasn't a very good day for SJ."

When they reach the room, they find SJ lying on her bed looking towards the television, which is not on.

"Hey kiddo, how are you feeling today?" Genevieve asks her daughter, "Granma's come to see you."

SJ doesn't move, but continues staring at the blank television.

Genevieve drops her stuff in the chair and comes over to sit on the bed next to SJ. Still, the young girl doesn't respond to her presence. Genevieve waves her hand before her eyes, but no response. "Kiddo? It's Momma." Still no response.

Genevieve rushes to the door and calls, "Nurse!"

The same nurse comes to the door.

Clearly afraid Genevieve's tears glisten in her eyes, "She's not responding. What's the matter?"

The nurse goes to SJ, checks her breathing and pulse, and spreads an eye to look at it.

"She's all right. I've seen this before. I think her body wants to help her mind cope with all that's going on. If you're patient, she'll come back to you." The nurse takes one last look at SJ. "If you want I can page Doctor Hamilton and ask him to come by."

"Only if he's in the building. You think this is common? She'll come out of it by herself?" Genevieve doesn't know what to think at this point.

"I think she'll come back soon, but I'll page the doctor and see where he is." The nurse reassures Genevieve and her mother who looks as worried.

Dr. Hamilton arrives at the hospital and goes directly to SJ's room. He notes that Genevieve and her mother are both there. SJ has gone into another staring fixation. He walks over close to the bed and claps his hands together, as loud as he can, just once. SJ jumps at the loud sound, but doesn't move for probably another minute. Then she slowly moves as if waking from a drugged sleep.

When she sees Dr. Hamilton she asks, "Is it time for another ordeal?"

Dr. Hamilton looks around for Granma and opens his hands in a gesture of 'well?'

Granma comes over to the bed and kisses SJ above the pirate patch over her right eye. "Would you like that, dear?"

SJ tries to shake off the lethargy that comes with her staring fixation, and finally moves to sit up against the headboard.

"I'm ready." She looks at everyone with her lone pirate's eye waiting for the story to begin.

Granma sits down on the side of the bed next to SJ and Dr. Hamilton. Genevieve sits on the chair, set in the reclining position for someone to sleep on it. Dr. Hamilton looks at Genevieve for a long moment, but she only focuses on her daughter and her health.

"Let me see, now. I may not get this all right as I only heard the one story." Granma begins.

SJ interrupts, "Ordeal."

"Oh, yes, ordeal is what you call it."

SJ instructs her in the rules, "The bear has to go through many ordeals to be worthy of a little boy or girl. This is the fourth ordeal."

"Oh. I didn't know that. Well a bear told me this story a long time ago, so I may not get it exactly right."

SJ interrupts again, "Is this the bear in the attic?"

"Yes, dear, it's that bear."

"Well he's a little bear so he must have been successful."

Granma looks to Genevieve and Dr. Hamilton, not understanding.

"There's a whole thing about that. I'll explain later." Genevieve reassures her mother.

"Oh. Okay. Please do." Granma turns back to SJ and begins, "The bear found itself in the deepest and darkest woods of Africa."

"Where's Ralph? Where's the Master of Ordeals? How was this one chosen?" SJ interrupts.

"Let me help you with this part, Mom." Genevieve volunteers. "Ralph woke the next morning after a full and restful night's sleep,

160

knowing he has completed three of his ordeals," she begins.

"You know I think there are seven ordeals." Dr. Hamilton inserts.

"Seven?" Everyone asks at once.

"Yes, I went back to Charles, my partner, and he talked to his children's bears and they told him they had seven ordeals." Dr. Hamilton informs them.

SJ shakes her head, "My poor bear."

"Well it's not as bad as all that." Dr. Hamilton responds to her, "But more on that later. Let's get on with the sto… the ordeal." Dr. Hamilton winks at SJ.

"All right, now where were we." Genevieve begins again. "Ralph woke up the next morning after a full and restful night's sleep. He knows he has completed three of the seven ordeals." Genevieve looks around the room to make sure there are no further dissenting opinions.

"So, Ralph the Bear goes to the Supreme Bear Council with his parents and waits as the Master of Ordeals selects the fourth ordeal from the Great Ordeals Mixer. When he takes the ball from the machine, the Master of Ordeals opens it and reads it out loud."

Genevieve looks to her mother for the name of the ordeal, but she doesn't understand so Genevieve asks, "What's the name of the ordeal, Mom?"

Granma, looks at her daughter with confusion, and suddenly she understands and says, "The King of the Jungle Ordeal."

Genevieve picks up the story, announcing: "'The King of the Jungle Ordeal.' There is a collective gasp that Ralph has selected such a deadly Ordeal. Only three bears have ever returned from the Jungle.

"Well anyway, Ralph looks to his father and says, 'I cannot do this, only three bears have ever returned from the deep and darkest jungles of Africa. And Ralph's father looks at his son and says, 'You have a little girl waiting for you to prove yourself worthy of her. I believe that you will find a way to survive the deepest and darkest jungles of Africa and come back to us. I have taught you many lessons, but the most important is to believe in yourself and to use your imagination to solve problems. I will wait for your safe return'. And Ralph turns to his mother and says, 'Mother I cannot do this, only three bears have ever survived the deepest and darkest parts of the jungles of Africa'. And Ralph's mother hugs her son and says simply, 'Your father and I believe

162

in you'.

"Ralph goes to the Master of Ordeals and asks how to get to the deepest and darkest parts of the jungles of Africa? And the Master of Ordeals responds, "You have to fly American to Gatwick, take the bus over to Heathrow and then catch the British Air flight into Lagos, Nigeria. From there it is an overnight train to the deepest and darkest parts of Africa. Ralph asks the Master of Ordeals, 'Are you paying for these tickets?' And the Master of Ordeals hands him the tickets he bought on Travelocity."

SJ gets upset, "Momma, you're being too..."

"Literal?" Dr. Hamilton inserts.

"Yeah, something like that." SJ concludes, looking for the story to progress.

"I'm almost ready to turn this puppy over to Granma." Genevieve begins, but SJ stops her, "It's not a puppy, it's a bear sto --, err... ordeal."

Dr. Hamilton smiles, "Gotcha."

SJ smiles, embarrassed that she was caught, but motions for them to keep going.

"So. Ralph the Bear has tickets to get to the deepest and darkest part of Africa. But confusion leads him to ask a question. So he asks the Master of Ordeals, 'What do I have to do in the deepest and darkest parts of Africa to prove I am worthy of my little girl?' And the Master of Ordeals says to Ralph, 'You have demonstrated the virtues of Courage and Humanity. In this ordeal you must demonstrate the virtue of Temperance.

"What's temperance?" SJ asks.

Genevieve starts to respond, but her mother picks up the story.

"Ralph asks the Master of Ordeals, 'Does that mean I have to avoid booze?' The Master of Ordeals tells Ralph, 'You obviously have much to learn. Go to the deepest and darkest reaches of the African jungle and discover the meaning of temperance.' And with that instruction Ralph kisses his mother and hugs his father good-bye and boards American flight fifty to London Gatwick."

Granma tries to think about how to make the story all fit together, but SJ is impatient, "Granma."

"All right child. Let's see now. The bear…"

SJ pipes up, "Ralph."

"Oh, yes, Ralph gets off the overnight train from Lagos in the deepest and darkest part of the African jungle, trying to figure out how he can demonstrate temperance."

Granma looks at Genevieve as if to say, 'Thanks a lot for nothing'.

"So the … Ralph, yes, Ralph the Bear wanders into the underbrush and sits down on an ant hill. Now the ants don't think much of this big old brown bear sitting on their hill so they bite him on the … bottom … and Ralph the Bear goes running to the nearest lake to wash off the ants that bite him on the…"

SJ pipes up, "Bottom?"

"So, we find our hero in the middle of a lake in the deepest and darkest part of the African jungle, washing biting ants off his …"

SJ giggles, "Bottom."

"Our hero, Ralph the Bear, sits in a lake wondering how to demonstrate temperance to pass this particular ordeal when along comes a Kangaroo."

SJ pipes up, "Granma, there aren't any Kangaroos in Africa."

Granma looks at her granddaughter and says, "Who says? You ever been there?"

SJ shakes her head.

"Then how do you know there aren't Kangaroos in Africa?"

SJ reminds her, "Books, Granma."

"Well you show me the book that says there are no Kangaroos in Africa and we'll change the story to a Wallaby."

SJ pulls her sleeve, "No Wallabies in Africa, Granma."

"How about a Bald Eagle?"

SJ shakes her head, "Don't think so."

"Well what would you suggest my dear?" Granma asks SJ.

"How about a Wildebeest? I don't know what it is, but Momma read about it to me once." SJ responds.

"All right. So our hero, Ralph the Bear, sits in an African lake, pulling biting ants off his bottom when a Wildebeest wanders by and

says to our hero, 'What's a fat old bear doing in the middle of my lake'?

Now Ralph didn't think of himself as fat or old, but he was willing to

forgive the Wildebeest for being so rude. He says to the Wildebeest, 'I'm

looking for an opportunity to demonstrate temperance. Do you know

how I could do that?' Now of course the Wildebeest had even less of an

idea as to what temperance meant than Ralph. But not to be

embarrassed by showing his ignorance, the Wildebeest replies, 'You

could convince the Lions not to hunt us Wildebeests.'

"Now Ralph the Bear, our hero, thinks this sounds like something

that would be good to do. He pulls the last ants off his bottom, climbs

out of the lake and goes looking for the King of the Lions. He traverses

dangerous terrain, hearing scary roars, and birds calling, and the

sounds of large cats snarling. Then he comes to the den of the King of

the Lions. So he knocks on the door and Misses Lion invites him in."

"Isn't that a lioness?" Dr. Hamilton asks.

SJ frowns at him so he shrugs.

Granma continues, "Yes, Misses Lion is also called a lioness. So

anyway, here's our hero, in the lion's den, at the invitation of Misses

Lion. He sees the lion cubs playing so he joins in their play, especially

since he is a very playful fellow. So Misses Lion watches as he plays

with the cubs. Low and behold, the King of the Lions comes home and

roars, 'What's this wimp doing in my house?' Now our hero spends the

better part of ten minutes looking for the wimp before he realizes the

King of the Lions is talking about him. Now the bear remembers he is

on a mission. He asks the King of the Lions why he hunts the

Wildebeest.

"The King says to our hero, Ralph, 'Lions hunt the animals that

would strip the land of its vegetation if we did not control the

population of such animals. And if the Wildebeests stripped the land,

then all animals would suffer and die of starvation. It's the natural

order that Lions must hunt those animals that would strip the land of

vegetation.'

"Now the bear thinks this sounds perfectly logical. So he asks, 'If

for some reason there were too many Lions, killing too many

Wildebeests, would it not make sense for some animal to come and kill

the Lions to put harmony back into nature?'

"The Lion listens to Ralph's question and responds 'Men do that, only they do it too well. There are no longer enough Lions to regulate the other herds.'

"Hearing this our hero, Ralph the Bear says to the King of the Lions, 'Oh mighty King, does it not make sense that if there are not enough Lions to regulate all of the herds that the Lions should choose fewer herds to regulate? Maybe they should leave the Wildebeests for man to regulate?'

"The King of the Lions listens to this argument. He agrees with Ralph the Bear, who is our hero, and says, 'Make it so, Mister Sulu. Full warp speed to the Klingon galaxy.'"

Genevieve observes, "I think you're mixing your metaphors."

Granma thinks about it for a moment, "Oh. Whatever. Anyway, Ralph the Bear, who is our hero, goes back to the lake. He tells the Wildebeest that the King of the Lions has agreed not to hunt Wildebeests. Now the Wildebeest is very happy that he will no longer need fear the Lions. The Wildebeest gives Ralph the Bear, our hero, a letter to take to the Master of Ordeals saying that Ralph the Bear, has negotiated a peace treaty between the Lions and the Wildebeests. In so doing, Ralph has introduced a measure of Temperance unknown in the deepest and darkest parts of the African Jungle.

"I think you need to finish this now, Genevieve since you know how it ends." Granma looks at her daughter with relief."

"Okay." Genevieve takes the handoff and looks at her daughter. "Now Ralph the Bear, our hero, just makes the day train from the deepest and darkest African jungle back to Lagos, Nigeria. He waits three days for a flight to Heathrow. Once he gets to Heathrow Transportation Security tells him that he has to put the letter from the Wildebeest into check luggage rather than carry it on because one never knows if it might not really be a letter bomb. The problem is that Ralph the Bear, our hero, didn't have any check baggage. So he has to leave the secure area, go into the outside world, buy an overnight bag, put the letter in it and then check it back in. However, he then must retrieve his bag and hand carry it on the bus to Gatwick for final passage home. He will have to check in his check bag with the letter one more time at Gatwick."

"Momma. What happens when Ralph returns to the Supreme Bear Council?" SJ impatiently waits for the end.

"So when Ralph the Bear, our hero, finally arrives home, he finds that his check bag had been sent to Shanghai by mistake. It would be delivered to his home in a week or so. At this point the Master of Ordeals tells Ralph the Bear, our hero, he will have to wait for the letter to arrive to be given credit for successfully completing his fourth ordeal. From what Ralph tells the Master of Ordeals, it appears he has demonstrated Temperance through forgiveness of the Wildebeest for calling him fat and old, humility and modesty for not claiming he negotiated the treaty all by himself, prudence for winning the trust of Misses Lion by playing with the cubs while the King was away, and self - regulation by proposing a scheme that works to the benefit of both the Lions and the Wildebeests. In addition, he demonstrated fairness in the terms of the treaty as no one is disadvantaged, and hope in that both the Lions and Wildebeests could hope for better futures under the terms and conditions of the treaty."

SJ looks up at her Granma, "What's the moral of this ordeal?"

Granma looks stumped. Dr. Hamilton suggests, "That you should not wait for someone to bite you in your bottom, before you get up off it and do something for others."

SJ smiles, "I like it. Ralph has completed four ordeals." SJ counts down the ordeals until her bear arrives.

"And they are the four most dangerous," Genevieve reminds her.

"So do I get number five tomorrow? It's your turn Doctor Hamilton." SJ asks.

Dr. Hamilton nods, "I think I can find Doctor Coolidge before that."

SJ smiles, but it fades quickly as she once again becomes tired. Dr. Hamilton notices and asks, "Looks like someone needs some sleep." He yawns to make SJ think he talks about himself. "Night all. Thank you for the sto... the ordeal Misses Wilcox. It was great." Dr. Hamilton waves to SJ as he leaves.

In the middle of the night SJ starts talking in her sleep. SJ's voice wakes Genevieve, asleep on the chair.

"Bad Granma, bad."

Genevieve raises her head to look around, but her mother has gone home for the night. "It's okay, kiddo," she whispers.

A moment later SJ thrashes about in her sleep and yells "Let him out!"

Genevieve gets out of bed and goes over to sit next to SJ.

The little girl moves her arms and legs under the covers as if she were in a fight with someone, "He doesn't want to be in your attic prison."

"It's okay; it's just a dream." Genevieve tries to comfort her daughter.

"The Gestapo is coming! They'll find him! Let him go now!"

Genevieve strokes her daughter's hair and finds it coming out in her hand in clumps. "Oh, no." She realizes the next stage has begun.

How do I explain this to SJ? She wonders.

SJ, still asleep, sits up suddenly with her eyes closed, "They're here for the bear. The Gestapo. We have to be quiet as mice or they'll find us."

Genevieve hugs SJ, but the little girl thinks it part of the dream and doesn't waken.

"They're in the house. Quiet. Quiet. Not a sound. Hold your breath. The lights! They're looking for us, for the bear. He's in the trunk under all those clothes, Granma never lets me wear."

Genevieve just holds her, waiting for the dream to be over.

"They found the door, they found the door! They're coming up. Hide everyone, Hide bear, deep in the trunk and they'll never find you. Oh! They're looking in the trunk, through the clothes; they're throwing the clothes all over ... Granma's going to be mad! Oh! They found the bear! They're taking him with them. No, bring him back, he's not your bear, he's for a little girl or boy. Please don't take him away!"

SJ cries at the loss of the bear.

"Don't be mad, Granma. Bears know how to overcome ordeals. He's a worthy bear. He got through his seven ordeals before. He'll get through this one."

SJ quiets down as if the dream ends. Genevieve lies her back down and brings the covers up, kisses her cheek and returns to her own uncomfortable chair bed.

The next morning Genevieve checks her hair and make-up in the bathroom mirror and rushes to SJ's bed. A quick kiss on the forehead of the child with thinning hair. "It'll be okay, kiddo. When the treatments are over it will all grow back." SJ grabs her mother around the neck for a hug. As Genevieve dashes toward the door, SJ calls out.

"Momma. Stay with me today."

Genevieve stops in mid-stride and turns in recognition and guilt at her daughter's pleading voice, even as she tries very hard to be early for once. "You know I would rather do that than anything else in the world, kiddo. But if I don't go in..."

"I know ... you could lose your job and your health insurance and I couldn't stay here until I get well..."

Genevieve returns to the bed for an extra hug and final kiss before she reluctantly follows the voice inside her head that says she has no other choice.

In the hall she nearly knocks Dr. Hamilton down as they both come around a corner from opposite directions at the same time.

Dr. Hamilton reacts first, "Sorry, my you look very nice this morning."

"Thanks, but I've got to hurry."

"Just a question."

She turns to look at him with an expression of dismay at not wanting to be later. He reacts to it but says nothing about it.

"A bear. What are you going to do when the seven ordeals are over?"

She doesn't want to admit this to him, but finally decides to, "Seven, you said there were seven ordeals. I have a bit of time yet, don't you think?"

"A week … maybe. She likes her ordeals."

"Yes, she does." Genevieve casts about for ideas, finally settling on the only one that seems feasible to her. "My car. I've been planning on selling it. If I can get enough for it then I can afford a bear."

"Don't you need it to get to work? To come here? Groceries, that sort of thing?"

"Well … I moved back into my mother's house. Busses run from there that can take me to work and here. It's not as convenient as a car, but I'm afraid I have run clean out of choices at the moment."

"But a bear's not that expensive."

"When you make as little as I do, a sole wage earner and a little girl in an expensive hospital like this, well…"

"Would you permit me…?"

"No! Absolutely not. You've already done much more than you should. You already made Bearmas come alive for her. Your ordeal started it all off. And now … I can't tell you how much it means to her."

Genevieve looks at Dr. Hamilton and holds his gaze, "Even in her dreams she talks about ordeals and bears being worthy."

Dr. Hamilton reveals his surprise, "I didn't know that."

"Last night, I heard her." Genevieve steps forward and gives the surprised Dr. Hamilton a hug, which he returns readily. He holds her longer than she expects. And for the second time in only a few minutes she regretfully pulls away and says, "Thank you," and she rushes off to work.

Later that morning, happily at work, Genevieve smiles at customers on the phone again for the first time in weeks. She moves right through her claims with her old efficiency. It's a good day and she won't let anything spoil it for her.

Janie comes in and dumps a whole list of new claims for her to intake. Genevieve picks up the list and goes to work on it before Janie gets back to her cubicle.

Within minutes Dean appears in her doorway and motions for her to come to his office. On the phone with a client, she holds up her index finger to indicate she will be only a minute.

"Yes, Mister Davidson, we can have your check ready by noon. If you'd like to stop by our Main Street office, you can pick it up. Yes, thank you sir and it has been great serving you today." She clicks off; Dean gives her a thumbs-up and nods for her to follow him.

When they reach his office he closes the door behind him and sits on the corner of his desk so he looks down at Genevieve. "Sounded like a good call. Customer was happy and I take it you didn't give away the farm."

"Nice man, very easy to satisfy."

"What's different today?"

"Dean?"

"The last several weeks you've been either not here physically or not here mentally. You're way behind on your calls, I'm getting complaints on your turn around time and customers have given you the lowest ratings in the department after being at the top for all those years. Yesterday was a real struggle for you and all of us. Today you're your old self. What happened overnight?"

"Bearmas. I'm going to sell my car and give my little girl a Bearmas. That will make her happy." Genevieve stares off into space, imagining what Bearmas could be like.

"You've lost me completely."

"Sometimes you get so far down in the bad things that happen you forget what's important. For SJ, Bearmas is important, and I know how I can give it to her."

"You know I had been dreading this meeting all week, because I thought I was going to have to let you go. But thankfully whatever this Bearmas thing is, it's made you happy. It's good to see the old you back. Now you can dig out and get back to number one. You need to or Andrea will have the ammunition she's been looking for."

Genevieve rises and gives Dean a quick hug and disappears out the door and back to her waiting clients.

The Fifth Ordeal: The Medusa in the Clouds

Genevieve pulls on her coat as she leaves work. Seven o'clock. The sun set long ago and a brisk wind causes her to shudder. The street lights cast shadows as she walks to her car. She notes the time realizing she arrived at seven in the morning with no lunch break. She made a lot of progress catching up on the most delinquent claims. Close to where she needs to be, she feels like her old self, only a lot more tired. She knows she took time from SJ to keep her job, but she still has to make enough to pay the bills. She really doesn't want to leave the insurance company right now. With SJ in the hospital she needs her income to pay the medical bills. If she couldn't pay, that would be disastrous for her. A declaration of personal bankruptcy inevitably leads an insurance adjuster to lose their job at Richland. That would also ensure that she would never work in the insurance industry again. It would ruin her credit so she couldn't rent an apartment or buy a car or anything.

She has few choices, none really. She can't go anywhere in the short term. She has to get out of her rut and start moving in a new direction. It has taken her a long time to come to this conclusion. Maybe it was her mother moving on. Maybe it was Janie coming in and ruining her perfect scenario. Whatever it was, she has finally made a decision to fix the thing that has been her biggest obstacle, herself. *Maybe this will be the end of one ordeal. Maybe it's the beginning of another.* She doesn't know for sure, but Bearmas has cleared much of her own thinking about life. It represents an opportunity to make SJ happy if only for a little while.

On the way home, Genevieve stops at a bookstore and buys a paperback book. It's a lot of money for this book, probably almost enough for a bear. But she knows she has to buy it. She has to study it and she has to start right now. She has already decided she won't eat lunch for the next month. That should be enough to cover the expense. She looks at her reflection in the store window. She decides losing five pounds won't make her look too thin.

Genevieve finds the nurses, Jacob and Dr. Hamilton waiting for her in SJ's room. She looks nervously around, "You're waiting for me?"

The charge nurse responds as the others nod, "Yup. You're late. SJ here's been waiting patiently for you. The doctor has been doing his best to keep us all entertained without spoiling the story you're going to tell ..."

SJ cuts her off, "The ordeal..."

Genevieve drops her things, kisses SJ on the forehead, "You ready, Kiddo?"

"I'm past ready. Ralph can't come until he gets through what... three more ordeals? And if he fails any one he has to go be a redeeming bear. Then I have to wait more than two whole years."

"Ralph's a courageous bear..." Genevieve starts.

"Momma." The message in SJ's voice is clear: Time to sit down and tell the ordeal. She complies, situating herself next to an anxious SJ.

Dr. Hamilton smiles at Genevieve. She begins to puzzle for a moment as if trying to remember how this goes. A look of remembrance crosses and she starts in.

"So when Ralph woke from a good night's sleep he returns to the

Supreme Bear Council with his parents and watches the Master of

Ordeals select another ball from the Great Ordeals Mixer.

When the Master of Ordeals opens the ball and reads the Ordeal to Ralph --"

"I hope this isn't too hard." SJ squeezes her mother's hand.

"The Master of Ordeals reads the slip of paper that says only, 'Bring back the jewel of the Sun God, Ra.' The other bears look to each other with very wide and fearful eyes. They had thought everyone had forgotten about the Sun God, Ra. But there is no rhyme or reason to how the Great Ordeals Mixer selects ordeals or the nature or difficulty of them."

SJ gazes off into the distance, as if trying to picture a large jewel in her mind's eye or at least that is what Genevieve thinks she is doing.

Genevieve continues, "Ralph looks to his father and says, 'Who is the Sun God, Ra? I don't know anything about him.'

"And Ralph's father looks at his son and says, 'Beats me, but I believe that you will find a way to recover the jewel of the Sun God, Ra and come back to us. Use your imagination to solve this problem.'

"Ralph turns to his mother and says, 'Mother, what do I do?' Ralph's mother hugs her son and says simply, 'Do as your father suggests.'"

SJ looks to her mother and says, "So how did he find the Sun God, Ra?"

Genevieve smiles at SJ, "I'm just coming to that. So the Master of Ordeals tells Ralph, "You do not go to the Sun God, Ra to find her jewel. It was stolen by the thirteen headed Medusa a thousand years ago. You must find the Medusa and retrieve the jewel."

"But how do I find this Medusa?" Ralph asks.

"'Your transportation awaits you outside.' The cryptic response from the Master of Ordeals confuses Ralph, but also makes him curious.

"Ralph doesn't know what to expect. A thirteen headed Medusa, a jewel stolen from a sun god he never heard of before. Transportation that awaits him. This poor bear has already been through so much to prove himself worthy of his little boy or girl. But he will not give up now. He must persevere.

"Ralph leaves the Hall of the Supreme Bear Council to find four long necked geese harnessed to a jewel-encrusted chair. He walks up to the nearest of the geese and asks, 'Mister Goose, I need to find the

Medusa in the Clouds. Can you take me there?'

"The nearest goose looks across to the other lead goose and remarks, 'Hey lefty, this guy wants us to take him to see the Medusa. You paid up your life insurance?'"

"The far goose rolls his eyes and shakes his head as if bears never get it right, 'Of course my insurance is paid up. I wouldn't leave home without it. But the Medusa is another thing all together, now. You remember the last time we took a bear up there? We hardly got away. And that poor bear. I can still see him with his long bladed knife trying to slay the Medusa, but not knowing which head to face. And then the tail came out of nowhere and sent him flying into the great beyond.'

"The near goose turns to Ralph with a look almost daring him to continue on this self-destructive voyage. But either Ralph doesn't believe the far goose or doesn't care. A little girl awaits. Ralph must prove himself worthy of her. Nothing, including a many headed Medusa and a blinding fast tail, can dissuade Ralph from his fate and his little girl.

"So Ralph climbs into the jewel-encrusted chair and looking straight ahead, says, trying to conceal the fear in his voice as best he can,

'Take me to the Medusa in the Clouds.'

"The geese, being magical geese, are obliged to do the bidding of whoever sits in that jewel-encrusted chair. As one, they lift off and carry Ralph skywards into the white fluffy clouds, leaving his mother and father watching him disappear from sight."

SJ has trouble picturing the Medusa. "How many heads does this Medusa thingy have?"

Genevieve stops to think about this for a moment, but Doctor Hamilton speaks up first, "She had thirteen heads on long flexible necks. So the heads actually turn and look at the other heads, move in front, to the side or even behind another head."

"That must be weird." SJ sounds like she doesn't completely buy Doctor Hamilton's explanation.

Genevieve doesn't know how much she should embellish this point so she appeals to SJ's logic. "Well ... anyone who lives in the clouds must be a little different from you and me."

"Does the Medusa have wings or something to keep herself from falling?" SJ still doesn't sound like she has the image clear.

"A long time ago people thought thunder was the gods having arguments and they lived up in the clouds. So I guess the Medusa was another of those supernatural beings that live up there amongst the gods." Genevieve explains. "So, Ralph keeps his head high as the four geese carry him to the cave of the Medusa. But as they make their way to the cave, Ralph looks down at the jewel-encrusted chair in which he rides. He notices that in front of him the jewels form a cross. He reaches out and finds that the cross is actually the handle of a magnificent sword. He withdraws the sword from its resting place and he discovers that in the very end of this handle is the largest dark red ruby he has ever seen."

"How big is that ruby?" SJ suspiciously asks her mother.

"As big as a ... tennis ball." Genevieve hesitates before deciding on something huge but also believable.

"You sure it was that big? Ralph must have big hands to hold that."

"Ralph wants to find this Medusa and he now thinks the geese have given him a magical sword with which to fight it."

"Is it magical?" SJ remains skeptical.

"You'll just have to wait and see, now won't you." Genevieve tries to keep the ordeal moving much to the chagrin of her daughter.

"I don't like to wait."

"None of us do, but Ralph is a patient bear. He would want you to be as well. So back to the ordeal. Ralph decides that if there is a sword, there may be other things hidden in the chair that can help him as well. He finds a gold shield beneath his feet. In the middle of the shield is a large smoky-grey, but transparent stone. As Ralph looks down he sees the ground a long way beneath him now, and his fear lessens. But just the same he doesn't remove the shield just yet. He wants something to rest his feet on until they reach the cave of the Medusa."

"Is he really afraid of falling?" SJ tries to follow the story.

"He's way up in the clouds by now, so yes, he is a little afraid, but more than that he doesn't want the Medusa to know all the things that he will use to fight her."

"I guess that makes sense." SJ relaxes and waits for her mother to continue.

"Anyway, Ralph continues to look around the jewel-encrusted

chair. He turns part-way around. He sees a carved helmet with a large red plume coming out of the top behind him. He reaches around to touch it only to find it is really metal and a real helmet. He stands up and puts his knee into the chair seat as he works the jewel-encrusted helmet loose and finally free. Ralph curiously notes that it is just his size. So still with his back to the direction the chair moves, he places the helmet on his head and raises the sword, whose gleaming blade sparkles in the sunlight.

"Ralph turns around to find the geese have arrived at the lair of the Medusa. They now fly into the mouth of the cave. It's very dark and scary in here. Sounds like moans and people suffering come to Ralph. But the sounds don't bother him. Or maybe he just doesn't know what the sounds really mean. Anyway, Ralph reaches down, now that they are in the cave that serves as the lair of the Medusa in the Clouds. He removes the jewel-encrusted shield from the floor of the chair. He holds it up and looks through the smoky grey stone."

"Why is he doing that?"

"Ralph has heard the stories of the Medusa from his father." Genevieve wants SJ to think of this like the stories she reads to her at night. She hopes SJ will make the connection as she doesn't want this to be too scary. It has to be an ordeal none-the-less.

"Did Ralph's father ever meet the Medusa?"

"No, but there are always legends. And this was the legend his father had heard."

SJ nods as she thinks about legends. Her mother gives her a moment before continuing.

"So why does Ralph look through the smoky colored stone?"

Genevieve knows SJ is ready for this part of the story now, "The legend is that the Medusa can turn a bear to stone with just a look from a particular one of her many heads. This head always has her eyes closed. She only opens them when she feels threatened. If she were to open her eyes and look around, she would most likely turn one of the other heads to stone."

"How can she turn things to stone just by looking at something?"

"Well, SJ, no one really knows. Anyone who was there was turned to stone and not able to tell anyone what she saw."

"Then how do we know the Medusa turned all those people to stone?"

"Maybe it was the geese from the jewel-encrusted chair."

"Maybe the Medusa likes to make statues." SJ suggests.

"Possible, but someone or something came back to tell the legend. And the legends said the Medusa just looked at a bear and was able to turn it to stone. So I guess until someone comes back with proof that isn't true we will just have to believe the legends."

Dr. Hamilton sees that SJ thinks about this. "Okay," arrives a moment later.

"So Ralph enters the lair of the Medusa in the Clouds. The geese land and wait for Ralph to exit from the jewel-encrusted chair, but he hesitates. 'This is as far as we may take you,' the near goose explains to Ralph.

"'Why is that?' Ralph asks the goose.

"'We are not permitted to enter the chamber of the Medusa, which lies just ahead. Only the bravest of the brave may enter there. We are mere transporters of those who would challenge the great and glorious

Medusa.' This sounds reasonable. So Ralph steps out of the chair, but hesitates before walking off to the chamber.

"'You will wait for me here?' Ralph asks the near goose, who looks across to his mate.

"'He wants us to wait for him Lefty. What should we do?'

"The other goose again rolls his eyes as if all bears are either naïve or stupid. He is not a mean spirited goose, in fact he really is just a silly old goose. So he agrees by saying, 'We can wait one hour at which time our meter runs out. Since I didn't bring any change I guess we will have to leave. Besides we must return for the next Medusan challenger anyway.'

"Ralph looks at the geese and has to ask, 'You don't bring many back, do you?'

"The far goose thinks for a moment before responding, 'Nope, can't remember the last one.'

"Ralph nods to himself, 'If I have not returned in one hour then you will be justified to leave me here, a statue like all the others before me.' And with that he holds the shield up, looks through the smoky gray stone in the middle and walks into the lair of the Medusa in the Clouds."

"Isn't he afraid? I am." SJ shivers. Genevieve gives her a hug to comfort her before continuing on.

"So Ralph noiselessly creeps forward keeping the shield in front of himself, hoping the smoky gray jewel will keep him from being turned into a stone should the Medusa open its eyes and see him."

"Why does he think the jewel will do that?"

"He doesn't know if it will, but he has to believe that the shield was there for a reason. Maybe he was the first to discover it, for if others had, he did not think that it would still be on the chair. It would be somewhere in the lair of the Medusa."

SJ looks at Dr. Hamilton who nods in agreement, so she turns back to her mother expectantly.

"As Ralph enters the room the first sight of the thirteen heads of the Medusa is more horrible than Ralph ever considered. The Medusa sleeps with each head lying on a pillow of silver threads. Each is uglier than the last. The smell of the unwashed monster overwhelms Ralph.

He stumbles and chokes at the same time. He makes enough noise that half of the heads rise up and open their eyes to see who enters the lair.

"Ralph regains his footing and raises the shield just as the many heads comprehend they have company. The many Medusa heads look at Ralph expecting something, but nothing happens. They gaze upon each other clearly confused and yet curious. Ralph steps one step closer. All of the open eyes of the Medusa return to him. And as they do, a strong rush of flame passes over Ralph's head. Ralph realizes that without his magical helmet his fur would have singed from the flames. He touches the helmet still on his head and finds that the fine red feather that had gloriously adorned it has vanished. All that remains is a thin spine of what had been the feather.

"Ralph scrunches down below the shield and watches the Medusa through the gray jewel in his shield. The Medusa has become more curious than before. Several of the heads extend on their long necks toward Ralph, as if to get a better look at this pesky presence.

"The head that approaches closest to Ralph bellows in a very loud voice, 'And who sent you to disturb our peaceful repose? No one has dared enter our lair in over a century.'

SJ's eye brows furrow. "How long is a century?"

"A hundred years." Dr. Hamilton responds, but Genevieve gives him a look and he sits back as if he understands her meaning.

"That's a long time." SJ remarks.

"Before you were born." Genevieve responds. She tries to restart the story but SJ stops her with a raised hand.

"You said the chair geese were returning for the next challenger, but no one has been there in over a century."

Dr. Hamilton raises an eyebrow. "Hmm, you're quite correct. It must be that the chair geese don't experience time the way we do. They are only dispatched when this particular ordeal comes up and apparently that doesn't happen very often."

"But there are lots of bears going through their ordeals aren't there?"

"Yes, but this must be a special ordeal that most bears don't go through."

"Is that good or bad for Ralph?"

Dr. Hamilton shrugs when Genevieve glances at him for support. "Neither. There are thousands of different ordeals that bears can go through. If everyone went through the same ones all of the time, they would no longer be ordeals now would they?"

"I don't know." SJ seems confused.

Genevieve goes back to the ordeal. "Ralph is not afraid … well … maybe a little. But he answers the Medusa right back, "I, Ralph the Bear, have come to reclaim the lost jewel of the Sun God Ra, of which you are in possession."

"One Medusa head moves closer to Ralph while half of the heads remain with their eyes closed. The same head then leans very near Ralph. She comes up right in front of the gray jewel in the gold shield that Ralph holds before him … well actually he shakes nearly uncontrollably behind it. He does his best to keep the Medusa in the Clouds from noticing. Ralph doesn't want to convey anything but confidence to the monster.

"Is the monster going to eat Ralph?" SJ wants to know.

"The Medusa usually just turns bears into something. Each head, according to the legend, has the ability to turn each challenger into

193

something different. But maybe … just maybe, one of those heads is a vampire head and would want to suck blood from his neck. Maybe another head wants to have a bear meat sandwich. With so many different heads, half of whom are still asleep, each with a mind of its own, it's really hard to know what the Medusa would or would not do. Anyway, the Medusa head looks at Ralph with just one eye through the gray jewel in the center of the gold shield. That one eye appears magnified through the stone. Ralph nearly drops the shield when that single huge eye seems to bore right through him.

SJ puts her hands to her mouth, fearful for Ralph.

"Getting a grip on things, Ralph straightens back up. He bangs the shield into the Medusa head, which causes it to recoil. Momentarily having the advantage of confusion, Ralph takes another step forward. This causes two more Medusa heads to open their eyes. As they gaze upon Ralph behind his shield, a mighty gale wind passes through the lair. Ralph drops his jewel-encrusted sword to hold onto the shield with both hands and brace himself against the fierce wind.

"Does the sword blow away?" SJ asks.

"No, with all of the jewels on the handle the sword is very heavy.

That keeps it from blowing away. But … the clattering sound draws the

curiosity of the Medusa. Three heads lean forward as the wind trails off.

Ralph instantly grabs the sword and pulls it in behind the shield so the

three heads can't see what he has. One head attempts to peer over the

shield, but Ralph lifts it and tilts it back to obstruct the Medusa's view.

"The Medusa head that tries to see over the shield asks in a very

high squeaky voice, 'What do you have back there, Mister Bear?'

"Ralph tries to steady his voice. He now remembers the story of

the quick tail that caught so many bears by surprise. He cautiously

looks through the jewel in the shield for any signs that the tail has been

sent to dispatch him. Relaxing for a moment, he remembers the

question and responds, 'I have only my wits about me.'

"What are wits?" SJ responds immediately.

"Wits are your ability to think quickly. If you can outwit someone

that means that you can think of something to defeat the other person

quicker than they can think of something to defeat you."

"I don't understand." SJ wants to clarify what her mother is

explaining.

"Ralph tries to outwit the Medusa and her thirteen heads. Concealing his magical sword was one of the ways he did that."

Genevieve continues. "So Ralph takes another step forward and asks the Medusa, 'What have you done with the jewel of Ra, the sun god?'

"The Medusa answers, 'It is well hidden, but in plain sight.' The Medusa pulls back the many heads and suddenly the other heads with their eyes still closed rise up. The one furthest back stretches its neck as high as possible. Two immense golden eyes slowly open and focus on Ralph. The bear looks through the gray jewel. He feels the temperature of the cave drop like a rock. The shield becomes encased in ice. Everything seems to stop moving. Ralph watches until the eyes close. At that moment he lifts the shield and rushes forward with the jewel-encrusted sword held high.

"Ralph finds himself directly in front of the startled Medusa who says, 'No one has ever survived the gaze of stone.' The Medusa seems quite perplexed especially staring at the spectacular sword pointed at the throat of the many heads. But then something quite remarkable happens."

"What?" SJ can hardly contain her desire to know the outcome.

"The Medusa looks at the jewel-encrusted sword and remarks, 'You hold in your hand the sword of Ra. The jewel you seek is the ruby on the handle.'

"A surprised Ralph turns the sword up-side-down to have a better look at the jewel at the base of the sword handle. A bright light fills the dark cavern. The light focuses itself through the bright red ruby turning into pure red light as it comes out the other side of the jewel. The red light bathes the Medusa. Before his eyes, the ugly Medusa slowly transforms into a beautiful young female bear with light brown fur and a red bow around her neck.

SJ looks in awe at her mother, clearly imagining this scene.

"The female bear looks down at herself and then at Ralph. 'I am Sadie. The Sun God Ra changed me into the Medusa more than a thousand years ago. All this time, all I wanted to do is to go home and be with my family.'

"Ralph looks sadly at Sadie. 'Bears don't live to be a thousand years old. Your family must be no more.' And Sadie looks sadder than Ralph ever saw any bear before. But then he has an idea, 'Sadie, I am going through my ordeals to become worthy of a little girl or boy who needs to be comforted. You have endured a thousand year ordeal. Come back with me to the Supreme Bear Council. Maybe they will help you find a little boy or girl that you can be worthy of. Then you will have a family.'"

SJ brightens at the thought, "Yes, Sadie needs a family, too."

"So Ralph takes Sadie by the hand and leads her back to the jewel-encrusted chair borne aloft by four geese. As they approach, the geese look at Ralph and Sadie. The goose nearest turns to the other and says, 'Lefty. I hope you waxed your wings because we got double duty going back.'

"Ralph replaces the shield into the floor and proudly helps Sadie up into the chair. Once she settles in, Ralph replaces the helmet above the chair and makes sure it is firmly in place. But Ralph doesn't return the jewel encrusted sword. He needs it to present to the Master of Ordeals and the Supreme Bear Council.

"As Ralph settles himself into the chair next to Sadie with the sword on his lap, he commands the geese, 'Take us back on your last flight. You shall never again need return to this place. The Medusa is no more.'

"The goose nearest turns to the other, 'How do you like them apples, Lefty? He's put us out of business. Guess we will just have to take that job at the Boston Commons as a Swan Boat.'

"Lefty looks back at the goose nearest and remarks, 'Had to happen someday.' And the four geese rise into the air returning to Earth for the final time, carrying a very happy Ralph and an apprehensive Sadie.

"Where's the Boston Common?" SJ seems to try to remember something.

"Remember the book, Make Way for Ducklings? I read it to you when you were little." Genevieve reminds her.

SJ considers for only a moment, "The Mother Duck and her ducklings that grew into swans." SJ remembers with a broad smile. But it lasts only a moment as SJ returns to the story. "But what happens to Sadie?

"The four geese deliver Ralph and Sadie to the Great Hall of the Supreme Bear Council. The Master of Ordeals waits for them to land.

Ralph climbs out of the jewel-encrusted chair first and helps Sadie out. He removes the shield with the great grey stone in the center and watches as the geese rise into the air, fly a circle around the Great Hall and wing rapidly towards Boston and the awaiting Commons Lake.

"Ralph introduces Sadie to the Master of Ordeals. All three enter the Great Hall together. Once inside, Ralph reunites with his mother and father. Both tearfully hug him once more, grateful he has returned to them. His mother asks, 'And who is this?'

"Ralph introduces Sadie, but speaks more to the Master of Ordeals than his parents. 'This is Sadie. She is far more worthy of a little boy or girl than I. She has endured a thousand-year ordeal.'

"'And what was that ordeal, Ralph the Bear?' asks the Master of Ordeals.

"Ralph presents the jewel-encrusted sword to the Master of Ordeals. 'This was the object of my ordeal. The jewel you seek is the ruby in the handle. It held the power to transform Sadie into the Medusa, which she became for ten centuries. I discovered it in the jewel-encrusted chair and took it into the lair of the Medusa. There, the sun's rays passed through the jewel once more and transformed her back into the bear she once was. And ten centuries as a thirteen-headed Medusa is an ordeal that should make her worthy without enduring further trials.'

"The Master of Ordeals listens carefully to Ralph's story. 'You speak eloquently, Ralph. The Supreme Bear Council shall take your recommendation under consideration. I cannot tell you what their decision shall be. I can only tell you that you have successfully completed your fifth ordeal. Your family is justly proud of your accomplishments. You have once again displayed virtues important to a worthy bear. And your modesty in speaking of the ordeal of Sadie has not gone unnoticed. It is time you rest and prepare for your next ordeal. It will far exceed the gravity of those you have endured so far. Return when you are ready for your most difficult and most severe test, yet.'

"Ralph wants Sadie to return with him to his home, but the Master of Ordeals leads her away. Both Sadie and Ralph shed bear tears at their separation."

SJ looks at her mother, "Ralph really likes her, doesn't he?"

"Yes, he does."

"Will he ever see her again?" SJ wonders.

"We'll have to just wait and see what fate they share, won't we?"

"I hope they meet again. Maybe they could share a little girl?"

"I bet you'd like that wouldn't you?" Genevieve confirms.

"Then Ralph wouldn't be lonely for other bears." SJ looks sheepishly at her mother, who gives her an affectionate hug.

SJ looks at Dr. Hamilton. "What was the moral of this story?"

"I like to think it's that you have the power to change your own fate in your hands. When everyone thinks you're doomed to failure, you still have the power to decide what to do and find a way to succeed."

"So I can get well, even if no one thinks I can."

"That's right SJ. You have that power. And Ralph will show you how."

"I liked that one." SJ remarks. "It was kind of scary, but in the end, Ralph completed another ordeal and helped others at the same time."

Dr. Hamilton's phone beeps, he looks at a text and rises abruptly, "Sorry all … I have to go visit another patient, but I wasn't about to miss my turn telling of Ralph's next ordeal. 'Night SJ. I'll check in on you in the morning. Jacob, the orderly will return you to your room."

Genevieve watches him go, sad that he has to leave so soon. She was hoping to talk with him for a few minutes and better understand the latest with SJ. That is not to be tonight. But it was a good day. SJ seems happy and she needs to get some sleep. Probably even more so than Ralph the Bear.

Genevieve rises as the nurses file out and the charge nurse and aide do the same. An orderly appears and wheels Jacob back to his room.

Jacob waves to SJ as he leaves. "Quantum physics." He reminds her.

SJ returns the wave still wondering what quantum physics might be.

Genevieve goes to the bathroom and starts to prepare for another night on the sleeper-chair.

SJ calls to her. "You like him, don't you?"

"Who, sweetheart?"

"Dr. Hamilton."

"He's nice."

"He tells great ordeals."

"Yes, he most certainly does."

SJ smiles as she scrunches down under her covers and turns over smiling all the way from her insides out.

Mid-morning the next day, Genevieve calls her mother from work.

"Hi, Mom. Would you do me a favor? I'm just flying through my claims today and if I work a little later than usual I should get nearly caught up. Could you stop by the hospital and stay with SJ for a while tonight?"

Genevieve's mother listens to the request, "No, dear, I can't help you tonight. I actually have a date."

"Mom, with SJ's condition ... is this really the time?"

"For what, Genevieve? Am I supposed to spend my whole life taking care of you and your child? I'm only just forty. I have a full life ahead of me if I go and find it, and I intend to do just that."

Sarcastically Genevieve responds, "Thanks, Mom." She hangs up and considers the turn of events. It's not like her mother had been keeping her desires a secret. She looks at the clock and realizes she can either work now or sulk about this and not get anything done. *Who was it? Scarlett O'Hara who said 'I'll worry about this tomorrow'? Or was it 'tomorrow is another day', or something like that?*

Genevieve places the next call. "Hello, Mister Walters, this is Genevieve Wilcox from Richland Insurance. About your claim..."

Eight o'clock and SJ checks the time once more. Her mother has not yet arrived. When she gets this late, a nurse usually comes in and tells her Momma is on her way but just held up in traffic, which seems to happen a lot.

SJ picks up the book on bears and comes to that same word, h-a-p-p-i-n-e-s-s. She looks at it for a long time. For some reason, that word, seems to be central to a lot of things in her life. It seems to SJ that *other than the nurse who always whistles and smiles I don't know anyone who is happy. Granma is not happy with me because of the bear. She's not happy with Momma, but I don't know why. Dr. Hamilton doesn't seem happy. I can see it in his eyes. But he should be happy. And the other grumpy old nurse isn't happy about anything.*

So it makes sense that if you're a nurse, half the time you're happy and if you're anything else, it doesn't look like it will happen. So why is this book so intent on making people believe everyone should be happy? Why do people want to be happy when most of the time they aren't? Even when Momma laughs, I never get the impression she's happy for more than that one moment.

What changes it from happy to happiness? And SJ spends the night contemplating that question.

Even when the nurse comes in much later and says, "Your Momma's working late and going to sleep at the house tonight – she'll see you in the morning," SJ doesn't really react to it other than go into one of her staring fixations. But this time, she is fixated on 'What changes it from happy to happiness?'

Through the night, in her staring fixation, SJ reviews everything she has seen, everything that has been read to her, and everything she has read. And from that she tries to find the answer to that one simple question.

The next morning SJ waits for her mother to come see her, but by eight o'clock she concludes she won't be coming this morning either. She picks up her bear book and keeps reading, past the happiness line to understand the rest of the story about how bears find happiness in the children they love.

SJ wonders, *does love have something to do with happiness? Is that what's missing in happy but present in happiness? Can you be happy without feeling loved?*

These are questions that are almost as important as why Granma doesn't have white hair. But then again, she gave herself until she gets back to school to figure that one out.

Dr. Hamilton stops by for his daily visit. "Good morning sunshine."

"Why do you always ask that?" SJ had never heard it before, but he uses it nearly every day.

"It's from an old song. Just an upbeat, happy kind of question."

There's that word again, happy.

"How do you feel today? You're looking pretty good." He observes.

SJ nods as one of the aides comes in to give her a bath. "I just don't understand happiness." She complains.

The aide doesn't look up and without even thinking responds, "It's the result of the metaphysical balance of the universe."

Dr. Hamilton responds, "What?"

"What's the difference between happy and happiness? Have you ever really thought about it?" The aide muses.

Dr. Hamilton drops his stethoscope and stares off into space. "Happy ... happiness. I'd say it has to do with the time horizon. Happy is short term, happiness is longer."

"Okay, I figured that out, but what does it mean? What does it take to be happy and what does it take to achieve happiness?" The aide continues the discussion.

SJ just looks at the two of them.

"Wow, that's a hard one." Dr. Hamilton responds as he considers it.

"Don't patronize me. Are you telling me that you don't know the answer?" The aide seems surprised.

"I guess I'm a situational theorist. It depends on the person and their situation. What I would do to achieve a happy state is different from what you or SJ or her mother would do. The same for happiness. My situation is different than you, or them." Dr. Hamilton seems to think he's answered the question, but his expression quickly changes as the aide calls him out.

"That's a cop out. Situational means there is no one answer and while I think there are variations on the theme there are central tendencies as to what makes people happy and what instills happiness." SJ realizes the aide doesn't intend to let him off easy, even though she is not following his argument.

"Wait a minute. Why are we having this conversation?" Dr. Hamilton asks.

"All I know is all of a sudden these questions pose themselves and I'm left here trying to solve them with only a limited frame of reference from which to extrapolate candidate solution sets." The aide responds. SJ hasn't followed anything since this conversation began.

"Why are you wrestling with these kinds of abstract problems?"

"Collective unconscious, whatever you want to call it, doc. I'm using it. But in the meantime, you still haven't answered my fundamental question about happy and happiness."

SJ thinks these two adults are talking about something that seems to confuse even them at the moment.

"All right. I'll have to think about it." Dr. Hamilton tries to conclude this discussion, when the aide continues, "Oh, and Doc, I wrote my Master's thesis on Sartre, Camus and the Death of Existentialism." Again the aide doesn't look up but continues getting things ready.

"So why are you working in a hospital as an aide?" Dr. Hamilton wonders aloud.

"It's like this, Doc. I went to school to figure out who I was and then to figure out what I wanted. I came to the conclusion that I'm nobody special and what I wanted was to help people without having to make decisions for them. So this is perfect."

"But with your degrees, you could do so much more."

"Possibly, but then I would be trying to make myself into someone I'm not and spend all day doing things that I really don't want to. Bottom line … I wouldn't be happy and what I did in a major part of my life would not lead to happiness. So changing beds and giving sponge baths is just fine." The aide looks at SJ who listens carefully. "I'll come back when you're finished here." The aide smiles at her and backs out.

Dr. Hamilton still seems lost in contemplation of this discussion when SJ pipes up, "Momma's afraid."

"What?" Dr. Hamilton has not transitioned from the last conversation.

"She's afraid she's going to be fired."

"Fired, like lose her job?" Dr. Hamilton tries desperately to make the change back and understand what SJ tells him.

SJ nods. "She's afraid. That's why she didn't come last night."

"Come here to see you?" Dr. Hamilton gets back on track, but still can't shake the happiness discussion.

"She needs to work late or she'll lose her job."

Dr. Hamilton puts more of the pieces of the puzzle together. "That why she's not here today?"

SJ nods, "She wants to be here, but she can't."

Dr. Hamilton considers alternatives, "What about your father, I've never seen him come to visit you."

"My father's dead."

"Dead dead, or just dead to your Momma and you?" Dr. Hamilton asks.

SJ doesn't answer that question because she doesn't understand it.

"Okay. Have you ever met your father?" Dr. Hamilton asks.

SJ shakes her head.

"Has he ever lived with you?"

Again SJ shakes her head.

"So it's just you and you Mom?"

SJ tearfully nods.

At work at the crack of dawn, Genevieve works through investigations on the latest intakes so she can leave not too late tonight and see SJ. She already feels guilty about not going yesterday or this morning, but she has no choice but to keep this roll going and get herself back into a current position with her clients. She knows she's afraid of spending too much time with SJ because the more time she spends with her the more time she wants to spend with her. And she has just not gotten comfortable around Janie. It's abundantly clear Janie sees her as a threat and would like to see her transferred elsewhere. But she's not about to walk away from what she built up over the last seven years because some new grad thinks she deserves it all.

The phone rings and she answers, "Richland Insurance, Genevieve Wilcox, how can I help you this fine morning?"

"Miss Wilcox, this is Doctor Hamilton over at the hospital. How are you this morning?"

"Is something wrong with SJ?"

"No, and maybe. I hope this isn't too much of an inconvenience, calling you at work like this?"

"No, no, please. What's the matter?"

"I had an extraordinary conversation with her and I'm still working through it."

"Did she tell you that you'd be happier as a janitor?"

"No, nothing like that. But the part I wanted to talk to you about is she mentioned that you weren't making it to the hospital to see her because you're afraid of losing your job."

"I came very close, but as long as I keep up I think I'm okay, at least for the moment. Anything else sends me into a tail spin, I'm

210

probably toast."

"I'm sorry to hear that." Dr. Hamilton waits a moment before continuing, "But do you think you could not discuss that with SJ? She really takes everything in your life and internalizes it, and I'm afraid it's slowing her progress."

"What are you saying? That you think I should not discuss my work and my private life with my daughter because it might upset her? Well from what I've seen the recovery hasn't even started. Everything you have done has had no effect on starting it. So how can my discussion of work have any effect on it at all?"

"Hold on, Miss Wilcox, I only want you to be aware of how much you mean to her. When you're depressed, so is she. And that does carry directly over on her spirit and willingness to fight this."

"That kid has more spunk than the both of us together. And besides, she's a big part of this life I'm leading; I can't just cut her out of it. "

"Miss Wilcox, the tumor is squeezing the life out of her unless I can stop or kill it. And I need your help to do that, I can't do it alone."

"What are you saying?"

"I'm saying that we're on the same team. If we work together we have a chance. But if we don't work together, then there really isn't any chance we can succeed in saving her."

"You know Doctor Hamilton, I hear what you're saying, but we're from two different worlds, you, and me and SJ. In your world the good guy always wins. In our world we have to fight and scrap for every inch of life we want to live. Nobody gives us anything. We don't have any advantages. We don't start from go, we start three blocks back and hope to get there before the starters lap the field. That's where we come from. You talk about taking trips to Chile. I can't even afford to buy their fruit in the grocery store. You apply the most exotic and expensive treatments to get the medical results you want to achieve. I have to move out of my apartment and move back to my mother's home to pay my portion of my daughter's medical bills. I'm sure something like that is inconceivable to someone like you who has it all and for whom nothing is impossible. For us, everything is impossible. When inconceivable is added to impossible we might as well commit suicide because we won't be able to recover in a lifetime."

Silence sits on the line until Dr. Hamilton asks, "Bad day?"

"I'm sorry. I came into work happy today because I figured out a way to give my daughter a Bearmas. And you're part of the reason I was able to do that. And now I'm dumping everything that I've had to overcome to get there. Please forgive me."

"Sounds like you're going through you own ordeals to get to her Bearmas" His tone softens. She notes an understanding that was not there when this conversation began.

"Only difference is mine are a lot harder to overcome."

"What can I do to help you overcome them?"

"You're already doing it. You're treating SJ the best you know how, you're contributing to the lore of the ordeal. What more could I ask?" She wonders what he could do that might make a difference.

"You can ask anything. I'll do what I can." His response comes across honestly.

"Cure her."

Friday night and Dr. Hamilton arranged to meet Michele after work for dinner. They meet at Taverna a restaurant he enjoys, partly because there is no band whose music they would disagree on. She has not given up on him yet, but he thinks the relationship hangs by a thread. He still has a tendency to talk about SJ and she has started talking more about her work. Maybe it's an accommodation; maybe it's just that she needs a place to dump her thoughts in an uncritical environment as well. Whatever it is, they are still together, still going to Chile in a few weeks and off to have an evening of food, fun and ultimately something more, if he doesn't say the wrong thing as he already has on more than one occasion.

He thinks one of Michele's virtues must be patience. That if put through an ordeal requiring it to prevail she would probably do very well. But then she knows all too much about bears and ordeals already. If he brings that up, the evening is bound to end earlier than necessary.

He sits at the table when she comes through the door, windswept long red hair, long legs, enticing mouth and twinkling eyes. *And this woman is a CFO?*

He rises to kiss her as she arrives, breathless, pulling him in with her lips and sending his body to tingling with a mere touch. As she sits, the waiter brings the Grey Goose Martini and the Dewar's and water that have become a standing joke between them.

They use them as a gage of the evening's success. If they get through without consuming the alcohol then they generally end the evening together. If either fails this simple test, then they seldom make it to dessert.

"Good day?" He asks mesmerized by how good she looks after a full day of crunching numbers and running auditors through meat grinders.

"We'll know shortly, won't we?" She sets the challenge for him.

He just sits and drinks her in for a few moments. He doesn't need to say anything as he surmises she enjoys his knowing look and the feel of his eyes upon her, the knowledge that the feel of his gentle hands may be soon in coming.

"Talked to Mauricio today. He has everything planned out for us and will even pick us up at the airport and take us to the hotel when we get in." He wants to start the evening looking ahead to the trip and what that means.

"Is he staying in the room with us?"

"Not sure he's old enough for the X rating."

The dinner conversations have grown very explicit in terms of building expectations of what will happen on this trip, but all predicated on his ability to pull the plug on his everyday life. He has already promised her he will not bring his blackberry, he will not check email at the hotel and he will not call the office to discuss the status of patients. That was the bare minimum she insisted upon. He has been trying to create some wiggle room around that, while she has been trying to get him to even leave his watch behind. He fought that suggestion saying he will need to know when to get to the airport if nothing else, and she reminds him all he really needs to do is tell Mauricio and it will be up to him to get them there in time. He hasn't agreed to this yet, but he already decided it is one of the things to give on to keep something else, like the right to respond to an emergency call from one of his partners.

Lately she raised the issue of where they will live afterwards. She hates his bachelor apartment. No taste is her simple characterization of the Spartan quarters he visits when not elsewhere occupied. They went there just once for a post dinner conjugal visit, which was not consummated. She spent the rest of their evening together inspecting his artifacts as if an archeologist trying to decipher what crazed sect could have ever encouraged someone to want to retain such a bizarre set of remembrances. He since went through and disposed of most of those items she critiqued.

She remains unwilling to return. She tells him she is more relaxed in her own environment and therefore more responsive to him. He has not been able to collect any information that confirms or refutes her claim, but he expects going to Chile will provide the evidence.

He also calls Mauricio nearly every day to talk about vineyards to visit and what wines they will need to sample and even talking about the best restaurants to visit on which days. The plan that evolves is flexible enough to address any contingency Dr. Hamilton can imagine. He also knows there are situations he has not contemplated and at least one will inevitably emerge. If he successfully meets her demands, the days will start later and end earlier. Mauricio prepares for that in the way he plans the day. Dr. Hamilton imagines this is not the first high maintenance party Mauricio has dealt with in his business. If he blows it … then Mauricio must adjust for one of two contingencies, more time tasting wines or an early departure to return. Minor transgressions result in more wines, just like the drinks at dinner and no conjugal visits. Major transgression and she is on the first flight and he follows the next day. She made it clear if the trip terminates early she doesn't want to have to put up with him for another eight hours trying to get home.

"You know I've probably put in more planning for the trip to Chile than they put into D day?" He notes as he peruses the menu, even though he knew what he would order when he decided to meet here.

"Then stop planning, leave poor Mauricio alone."

"I'm having the…"

"…Fiocchi, I know." She finishes his thought.

"And you're having…"

"…The Risotto Pesche, of course."

"Would you like to skip this part of the evening and go right to the Grand Finale?" He feels awkward, as if still in audition mode and that one misstep will cause him to lose the part.

"A bit eager tonight, are we?"

"Actually I'm not as hungry as I thought."

"But the Fiocchi isn't a large dish."

"No, but filling."

"I'm famished, so you'll just have to be a good boy and wait your turn."

"So, how about them cowboys?" He wants to get her attention.

"Didn't know it was football season."

"It's not, but the rodeo's in town." He watches as she looks up from her menu and parts those lips just so. He knows she knows what fires his ardor and will keep him in line until she's ready for him.

But not tonight. He focuses on her eyes. For what seems to him to be the first time, they tell a different story. Or maybe it's just that previously he hadn't taken the time to look.

The waiter comes and takes their orders. When he leaves, Dr. Hamilton follows his curiosity and looks deeper into Michele's eyes. He doesn't say a word, but just drills deeper and deeper into the hidden recesses.

At first she takes this as a compliment. Just lets him try to ferret out whatever secrets he can find in there. But as the silence builds, she becomes more and more uncomfortable. She wets her lips, trying to draw his attention, but it doesn't work. She looks away to disrupt his efforts, but when she looks back the drilling continues.

Finally in an annoyed voice, "What is it with you tonight?" She leans across the table and stares as deeply into his eyes as she can see.

The waiter comes with the food. She thanks him and looks at her risotto. He still stares into her eyes, but now she will not look back at him.

"Better eat or it will get cold." She advises as she takes a forkful.

He sits there staring at her while she slowly and deliberately consumes her meal, including a glass of New Zealand Pinot Noir. She passes on dessert and finally looks back at him and his full plate of Fiocchi before him.

"You said you weren't hungry, but the least you could do is box it and take it home." She recommends, but now he engages her eyes once more, and for the first time this evening she looks into his eyes and finally understands what he is looking for.

She relaxes and leans back in her chair.

"Maybe I'm not ready to let you in yet, not totally and completely. I don't know what you'll do with some of the things you'll find in there. I surprise myself sometimes." She smiles as if in remembrance of something. "This really will be a two way audition. You might pass with flying colors and I'm the one who might not make it."

She stands up and gathers her things. "Shall we go?"

He pays the bill with cash and looks up at her, "I'll take a rain check tonight. I think it might be better to give us a little time."

The lips draw together. The eyes lack the confidence with which they started the evening. The tide has turned and now he has some decisions to make.

The Sixth Ordeal: Lotus Eaters

Dr. Hamilton paces around the room talking on his cell phone.

SJ sits up in her bed, waiting for her mother to appear. The charge nurse and the aide who bathes SJ sit on the chair-bed.

Genevieve appears in the door. A smile comes across her face as she sees SJ sitting there watching her with her one eye. "Must be time for an ordeal," she remarks.

"Yes. And Doctor Hamilton's been waiting for you so he can start. Sit here. Ralph's getting anxious." SJ pats the bed next to her.

Genevieve nods to the nurse and the aide as she sets her things down. She squeezes Dr. Hamilton's arm as she walks past him and as he hangs up his cell phone. She kisses SJ on the forehead and she settles in next to her.

"Let me see. Another ordeal for poor Ralph the Bear. Let me think a moment. It indeed has been a while since I thought about this." Doctor Hamilton begins.

"So with a good night's sleep he returns to the Supreme Bear Council with his parents. He watches the Master of Ordeals select another ball from the Great Ordeals Mixer.

When the Master of Ordeals opens the ball and reads the Ordeal to Ralph --"

"I can't listen to this part. Tell me what it is later." SJ puts her hands over her ears.

"The Master of Ordeals reads the slip of paper that says only, 'Convince the King of the Lotus Eaters to help others.' And every bear gasps in horror for no bear ever returned from this dreaded ordeal."

SJ removes her hands, "What's a Lotus Eater?"

"You heard, you little stinker." Genevieve tickles her daughter who breaks out laughing as she tries to push her mother's hands away.

"Well anyway," Dr. Hamilton continues, "Ralph looks to his father and says, 'I cannot do this. No bear ever survived an encounter with the Lotus Eaters.

"And Ralph's father looks at his son and says, 'I raised you to do what is right and what is important. You have a little girl that waits for you to prove yourself worthy of her. I believe you will find a way to visit the Lotus Eaters and come back to us. I have taught you many lessons, but the most important lesson is to believe in yourself and to use your imagination to solve problems."

"Ralph turns to his mother and says, 'Mother I cannot do this. No bear ever visited the Lotus Eaters and returned. And Ralph's mother hugs her son and says simply, 'Your father and I believe in you.'"

SJ looks to her mother and says, "Where do these Lotus Eaters live?"

Dr. Hamilton continues, "So the Master of Ordeals tells Ralph he must find the deepest and darkest part of the woods for the Lotus Eaters live somewhere in that dark and mysterious place."

"Ralph leaves the Hall of the Supreme Bear Council puzzled by the challenge of finding the King of the Lotus Eaters. First of all, he doesn't know where the Lotus Eaters live, and he has no idea how to identify the King, even if he finds him. This time the Master of Ordeals was less helpful in pointing him in the direction he must take. Ralph thinks about that for a long time as he walks along. He suddenly realizes he doesn't know where he is. The road is unfamiliar. The forest is denser than he can remember ever seeing. It is so dense he cannot see light even just a few feet off the road. Now Ralph is an observant bear. This makes him wonder why light doesn't penetrate the canopy of trees overhead. So Ralph looks up. He sees that the trees are much taller than he remembers seeing in the other parts of the forest where he grew up. Ralph looks around him wondering if the tall trees are just in this one location. He sees they extend as far as he can see."

SJ makes a face, turns to her mother and asks, "Why are the trees so tall?"

Genevieve smiles and responds, "We will all just have to wait and see, now won't we?" This doesn't satisfy SJ, but the faces stop and she returns her attention to Dr. Hamilton.

"So Ralph stops and listens to the sounds of the forest, realizing the normal wind rustling through the leaves is missing. In fact, a strange silence surrounds the bear. This causes him to scan the darkness looking for anything that will provide him a clue as to what he needs to do. Ralph stands in the middle of the road. He opens up all of his senses to detect anything nearby. It's not a sound he reacts to. It's not something that he sees, either. What he reacts to is a feeling. A feeling that something watches him. That something prefers to remain hidden, to study him, to come to understand him without revealing anything about itself. Ralph has a choice to make. He can either, watch and wait for the unseen presence to reveal itself, or let it know he knows it is there. He wants to engage it on his terms. Being a decisive bear, he chooses the later. He calls out, "Hello, I'd like to talk with you." Ralph looks deep into the darkness, not knowing if this is where the unseen presence lurks.

"Ralph now waits patiently. His patience is soon rewarded. At first he doesn't see her as she dresses entirely in black. She moves very slowly. But soon her white face appears almost like a ghostly image suspended in the black forest directly in front of him. Ralph's eyes widen as he watches more and more of her become visible. She finally steps from the forest onto the road. 'I am Lorelei.' This beautiful woman with long black hair, expressive eyes and a silky voice almost sings her name.

"After a moment to take her in, Ralph recovers and responds, 'I'm looking for the King of the Lotus Eaters. Would you happen to know where I might find him?'

"Lorelei blinks rapidly a few times. She refocuses on Ralph. 'The King died a long time ago.'

"Ralph considers this for a moment before responding, 'That will make my quest even more difficult.'

"Lorelei turns her head quickly as if she hears something. She dismisses it and turns back to Ralph. 'And what is your quest brave bear?'

"Ralph looks into the forest to see what caught her attention, but he sees nothing there. He looks hard expecting to see at least another floating face. But nothing can be seen. 'My quest is to find the King of the Lotus Eaters.'

"Lorelei nods understanding part of the dilemma, but not all. "And once you found the King, what did you expect to happen?'

"Ralph suddenly becomes wary of the silky voice. He decides to answer cautiously. 'The Supreme Bear Council sent me on this quest to ask the King of the Lotus Eaters to help us with a matter that I can only discuss with the King.'

"Lorelei's voice becomes even silkier, or so it seems to Ralph. 'I can take you to our Grand Counselor. She will know what to do.'

Again, Lorelei becomes distracted by something in the forest that causes her to turn slightly. Ralph's eyes follow hers. This time his gaze is rewarded. A dozen floating faces gradually appear all around him. The others do not emerge as Lorelei has, but rather remain only an apparition, or so it seems to Ralph."

SJ cannot wait longer. "What's an appa-whats-it?"

Dr. Hamilton nods in understanding of her confusion. "An apparition. It's something that appears before you. It generally isn't real, just something that you think is there. It often is your mind playing tricks on you."

"How does my mind play tricks on me?" SJ curiously responds.

"Lots of times when you're in a hurry you may only see part of something, so your mind completes the image. How it does that may or may not be the way the image really looks."

"Like what?"

"Well … if you were to glance up at clouds in the sky, you may see what looks like a face. What you're really seeing is a shape of clouds with some of the same outlines as a face. But your mind fills in the blanks to make it fit patterns you expect. If you look at that cloud closer, you realize the pattern is far from complete. The cloud really doesn't look like a face. And as the winds blow, the clouds change shape. They begin to look like something else, which may suggest some other pattern that you have stored in your brain."

"But what does that have to do with an app-a-whatcha-ma-call-it?"

"The apparition is something that, like the clouds, appears to be there, but really isn't. In this case Ralph thinks the floating faces are just an apparition, but in fact, they are real and they are there."

"How does Ralph know that?"

"Just listen." Dr. Hamilton continues the story. "Lorelei nods to the faces in the forest. One-by-one they wink out like stars in the early morning sky. And then it is just Lorelei and Ralph standing on the road, facing each other expectantly. Then Ralph remembers and asks, 'Who is your Grand Counselor?'

"Lorelei returns her full attention to the bear. 'She was the wife of our late dead King.'

"Ralph puzzles for a moment, 'But wouldn't that make her the Queen?'

"Lorelei answers simply. 'No, she was not the Queen. Please come with me as soon the sun will set. It is not safe to be here then.'

"Ralph decides there is much he does not understand. He needs to learn more in order to complete this ordeal. 'Why won't it be safe after sunset?'

"Lorelei takes his paw and leads him into the dark forest. She answers his question only after they have lost sight of the road and the light that shone upon it. Now it is so dark Ralph cannot see his guide. He can only follow along behind, led by the firm pressure on his paw. 'Perhaps she will show you what lurks in the night. Perhaps she will spare you. If I were you, I would not be too eager to know the unknowable.'

"Ralph holds on tightly to Lorelei's hand, realizing that if they were to become separated he might never find his way back to the road. He might also encounter whatever it is that lurks in these woods, making it unsafe after sunset. But Ralph wonders what the sunset has to do with it. It's as dark as night all the time in this strange forest."

Dr. Hamilton sees SJ shudder at his description of the dark forest and the realization that she is relating to the danger drives him on. "Without warning, Lorelei moves faster, dodging trees and other obstacles. Ralph is not used to running just on his hind legs. He finds his little legs pumping furiously to keep up. And still she goes faster. Ralph clings to her hand, afraid he will lose his one thread to hope and finding the Lotus Eaters. But now Lorelei moves so fast that Ralph's feet don't always touch down as she pulls him along like a rag doll.

"Ralph clasps her hand with both of his front paws. Now one of his hind feet only touches down once in a while. The bear wishes she would simply stop, pick him up and carry him with her. But he is so out of breath he can't ask the question. He feels his little heart pumping away furiously. He becomes afraid that if she doesn't slow down soon it just might burst.

"Turning his head, Ralph sees other white faces moving through the forest like ghosts upon unseen black stallions. He thinks he might be hallucinating, but he remembers the dozen or so others that appeared at the road. He realizes they are traveling with them to the destination. To see the Grand Counselor, whoever she is. To come to a resolution of his quest, however that will come out. Maybe they are just along for the

227

entertainment. Maybe they just want to see what she will do to him. *Do these people eat bears?* The thought catches Ralph by surprise. He had never considered that before. And the fact that he doesn't know if people eat bears worries him. But he feels like he is losing his grip on Lorelei. He pushes harder on the rare occasion that a foot really does touch down. He attempts to ease the strain on his grip, but it doesn't help. He tries to call to her, but he is so out of breath nothing comes out. He tries squeezing with all of his strength ... to hold on, hoping that they are near the end of this particular journey. He only wants to rest.

"And then as Lorelei swings to her left to avoid a tree or some other unseen obstacle. Ralph thinks he sees a glimmer of light. But it's not the light of the sun. It looks more like the light of a fire. *It would have to be a big fire to generate that much light.* But Ralph is not sure if it's real or his mind playing tricks on him. He fears it might be another apparition, like the others that proved to be real. He hopes against hope that this one is real as well.

"A turn to the right and there it is again. The apparent fire is bigger ... closer now. Ralph becomes more optimistic that it might be real. Still he has to grit his teeth to hold on to Lorelei's hand. He has to concentrate with all his strength, both mental and physical. He closes his eyes. He's surprised that it doesn't seem any different ... pitch black ... so he opens them again and catches still another glance of the light up ahead. Now Ralph is sure they are approaching something ... the destination, he hopes. And only now, for the first time Ralph realizes he will be dependent upon these people to lead him out of this place. He has absolutely no idea how he got here or even where here is.

"Lorelei begins to slow. Ralph's feet touch the ground much more often, although they still spin like a windmill, hopping and bouncing along. And still she slows more. Soon Ralph is merely running along like any other bear pulled along by a fast moving human.

"The fire illuminates a large structure, of which Ralph can, only just barely, make out the outline. There seems to be a large chair on the other side of the fire, as if this were the place where someone watches the fire. *But why would anyone want to sit and watch a large bonfire?* Ralph now trots behind Lorelei. With a turn of his head he can see the others are in fact quickly walking in the same direction, that is, directly to the bonfire."

"Who are the others?" SJ wants to know.

"Wait and we will get to that." Dr. Hamilton reassures her. "As they walk into the light aura of the fire, Lorelei releases Ralph's paws. He stumbles and falls facing the flames. Lorelei turns to look at him, but doesn't offer any assistance. In fact, she backs away and melts into the shadows. Ralph senses there are many more people about, but that they are also hanging in the shadows, not wanting to reveal themselves or their numbers to this uninvited guest."

"Why don't they want Ralph to see them?" SJ demands.

"Because they can better control the situation when Ralph doesn't know much about what's going to happen." Dr. Hamilton explains. "So Ralph lies on his tummy in front of the fire. No one else can be seen."

"Ralph gets up and brushes the dirt off his fur as he waits to see what will happen next. It's less than a minute before another woman, who looks very much like Lorelei, but her hair seems shorter and her face seems more round, at least to Ralph, stumbles into the firelight, and falls to the ground. Three more women, all dressed in black, all with long black hair, and carrying long rods with a small decorative cap, follow her and stand over her with a menacing posture. The woman on

230

the ground sits up. She glances at her guards, pulls herself into a Yoga-like sitting position and apparently begins to meditate.

"Everything is quiet, but there is a sense of anticipation. Ralph can see it on the faces of the guards. He can sense it even in the woman who waits. She meditates, but Ralph senses this is only something to do while she waits. It's not long before a trumpet blares a strange tune. In a moment a red-haired woman, slightly larger than the others, but just as beautiful, enters the light. She climbs up into the chair on the other side of the fire.

"The red-haired woman calls in a commanding voice: 'What has Andrea done?'

"One of the guards raises a branch with round green leaves as she talks. 'Andrea refuses to eat of the Lotus plant. She claims she no longer needs a false reality. In fact she claims the world is a beautiful place without the prism of the plant showing us the inner sanctity of life.'

"The other guards chant in unison, 'The prism of the plant shows us the inner sanctity of life. It gives us order and purpose and strength to protect our reality from those who would steal it away.' All three guards bang their rods on the ground in unison, three consecutive

231

times.

"The first guard raises the branch once more. 'She is a heretic. She believes that the plant that is the source of our altered consciousness is not divinely created.' A collective gasp fills the air, coming from a crowd of unseen observers who Ralph estimates must number in the hundreds. 'She is a heretic for she believes it is we who have created a false understanding of our world. She suggests that the larger world reflects a diversity of beliefs, all embraced by the one true God, who leaves us here only to find a way to live together in peace and harmony.'

"The other guards chant in unison, 'The prism of the plant shows us the inner sanctity of life. It gives us order and purpose and strength to protect our reality from those who would steal it away.' All three guards bang their rods on the ground in unison, three consecutive times.

"The first guard raises the branch once more. 'She is a heretic. She believes that men are equal to women and should be given equal responsibility along with their freedom.' A second collective gasp rises from the unseen one hundred or so shadows.

232

"The other guards chant in unison, 'The prism of the plant shows us the inner sanctity of life. It gives us order and purpose and strength to protect our reality from those who would steal it away.' All three guards bang their rods on the ground in unison, three consecutive times.

"At this Ralph raises his paw, but is ignored by all those whom he can see. 'Excuse me? Might I ask a question?'

"The red-haired woman turns and notices Ralph for the first time. 'And who is this bear? Who brought him to our forest home?'

"Lorelei steps back into the light from the shadows. 'I did Grand Counselor. He is sent by the Supreme Bear Council to ask your help.' Lorelei bows her head and steps back into the shadows.

"The Grand Counselor turns away from Ralph and back to Andrea. 'One thing at a time. The next you know we will have to multi-task, again. That was our downfall, thinking we could do everything a little at a time and get everything done. That fallacy has been demonstrated. We are now stronger and in control because we learned the power of One Thing at a Time. We have rendered men subservient by forcing them to multitask. They are incapable of doing it all, just as

233

we were. And their inability to succeed has been the secret of our rise to power. Now we dominate them by day ... but enough. Andrea. You are a heretic. You would have us abandon the true life to return to the reality we chose to leave those many centuries ago. The Lotus plant gives us our power. It gives us our strength. It gives us insights into the world that the other creatures of this world cannot dream of. Why would you have us abandon that which makes us great? Why would you have us embrace those who have false gods and false beliefs? Why Andrea?'

"The woman on the ground opens one eye and stares straight ahead. After a moment the other eye opens and she eventually looks up at the red-haired woman. She rises to her feet and stands defiantly before her and the three guards with their long rods. 'History is full of those who disbelieve. Sometimes they are proven wrong. But in all too many cases we find it was indeed the rest of the world that was wrong. Our society is built upon a dream. This dream is chemically induced. It clouds our perceptions of reality. You say that the Lotus makes us free, but I disagree. I have voluntarily chosen not to eat the Lotus any more. I have been able to see the world through my unimpaired senses. I see there is much that is not good. I see that not everyone is beautiful. I see things should be different. But not my sisters who are slaves to the plant and the prism it makes us view the world through. I say we have the opportunity to be free. Really free. Of the tyranny of the plant. Of the tyranny of false dreams. Of the fear that we all live in of the night, even though we live an existence darker than the night, and more fearsome.'

"The red-haired woman rises from her throne. 'My late husband, our King, made us his slaves. We threw off the yoke of male dominance. We have returned the Lotus Eaters to the matriarchal society that predominated for thousands of years before men found a way to overthrow us. If we give up the Lotus life, men may find a way to regain the upper hand as they once did. Our chemically induced society is the only true life. We cannot go back. We cannot permit heretics in our midst. Andrea, you are my sister, but we cannot permit you to preach a false gospel that may tear our society apart. You must suffer the consequences of your departure from the one true path.'

"The guards chant in unison, 'The prism of the plant shows us the inner sanctity of life. It gives us order and purpose and strength to protect our reality from those who would steal it away.' All three guards bang their rods on the ground in unison, three consecutive times. Then they take Andrea by the arms. They lead her to a stairwell.

Climbing to the top they come out on a terrace that overlooks the courtyard below. The bonfire is directly below. The guards push Andrea, who falls into the fire. She is instantaneously consumed by the roaring flames. Andrea's screams rise to a pitch for only a few moments and then die away."

"Why did they do that?" SJ has tears in her eyes as she looks back to her mother.

"Some people are not tolerant of others who are not like them." Genevieve tries to explain, but she sees SJ isn't satisfied. "You know how when you're sick people stay away from you because they don't want to catch what you have?"

SJ nods.

"Well in this case Andrea had an idea disease that they didn't want others to catch. They were afraid it would threaten them."

"Was Andrea sick?" SJ tries to understand.

"The red-haired woman thought she was."

"But why did they burn her?"

"Do you remember our discussing the witches of Salem?"

SJ brightens, "Oh, yes. The witches made everyone afraid."

"What happened to the witches?"

SJ sounds more somber remembering, "They burned them."

"The red-haired woman thought Andrea was a witch of sorts."

"But you said those women in Salem weren't really witches."

"They weren't. But people were afraid of women who were different. When they were at a loss for explanations for things that happened, they attributed them to the women and the witchcraft they thought they performed."

"So Andrea wasn't a witch?"

"No, dear. She wasn't a witch. Just someone who believed something not popular with those in control."

Dr. Hamilton nods upon the conclusion of this discussion. "Are we ready to get back to the story?"

SJ turns back to the doctor and waits for him to restart.

"Dr. Hamilton winks at Genevieve, "Okay. So here is Ralph standing next to a bonfire where one of the women has just been burned for not sharing their beliefs. Of course Ralph is a little nervous about being the next into the fire. He tries not to show it. He raises his paw again. 'Excuse me? Can we move on to the next thing now?'

"The red-haired woman turns her gaze upon the bear and in that same commanding voice responds, 'Now who are you?'

"Ralph does his best imitation of a gracious bow. 'Ralph the Bear at your service. I was sent by the Supreme Bear Council to ask your help.'

"The red-haired woman looks in the shadows for Lorelei. She stares for a moment. Lorelei comes out of the shadows and bows her head before speaking, 'Yes, Grand Counselor'

"The red-haired woman sounds contemptuous, 'You brought a bear to me without knowing what he truly wants?'

"Lorelei keeps her head bowed as she responds, 'A bear is not sly like a fox. Nor is a bear merciless like a tiger. A bear is honest. When he says he wants our help, I believe that we should accept that as true.'

The harsh gaze of the red-haired woman leaves Lorelei and

returns to Ralph. 'So mister bear, you have beguiled at least one of our

number. What is the help you seek from the Lotus Eaters?'

"Ralph hesitates as he thinks about how to make the request. He

decides there is not one good way to ask and simply does. 'Bears

comfort sick children.'

"The harsh gaze of the red-haired woman lessens. She listens with

fewer resistances. 'We are aware of that. We sometimes have sick

children of our own. Your cousins are a great comfort to them.'

"The lump in Ralph's throat eases. He finds he can talk easier. 'But

many times the sick children experience severe pain or emotional

disorders which are very difficult to calm. There is a shortage of

medicines that help these very sick children. And in some instances

their parents cannot afford the medicines that are available.'

"A nod of the head indicates the red-haired woman understands.

'We treat our children with the fruits of the Lotus blossom. This eases

the pain and helps even the most distraught child calm down and heal

the underlying cause.'

"Ralph knows he has to ask the question which the red-haired woman has alluded to, possibly without realizing it. 'The Supreme Bear Council would like you to donate your Lotus blossoms to the poor and needy sick children who cannot afford the treatments that would otherwise be available to them.'

"The red-haired woman instantly rises and looks over the flames at Ralph. 'You cannot be serious. Our society is dependent upon the fruits of the Lotus blossom to maintain our peaceful nature. We were once fierce tribes who regularly killed members of the neighboring tribes to right some slight or imagined wrong. Since we began to eat the fruits of the Lotus blossom there have been no wars, no crime and no strife amongst us. You would ask us to give this up so you can ease the pain of young children whom we do not even know?'

"Ralph nods his head."

"A consultation with the shadows brings the red-haired woman's attention back to Ralph. 'How is your proposal any different from what Andrea suggested just before we burned her in the fire?'

"Ralph also consults the shadows, although he is unable to see anything in them. He has the clear sense they are all there and waiting for his response. The wrong response and Ralph knows he will be joining Andrea in the fire. 'It's different because I'm not saying your

beliefs are wrong. I'm not trying to say that I have a better set of beliefs

or even a different set of beliefs. What I'm asking is for you to expand a

belief you already have … that the fruits of the Lotus blossom can help

sick children in pain or who are suffering. I'm asking you to rise to a

higher purpose. That you look beyond yourselves. Help ease the pain

and suffering of children, who through no fault of their own, find

themselves having to deal with something that each of us would have a

difficult time handling.'

"The red-haired woman doesn't wait before her response. 'Out of

the question. We cannot give you what you want without destroying

that which we have created. There are only so many Lotus blossoms.

We have none to spare. No, mister Bear. You must find someone else to

help your children in pain. We will not help you.'

"At this, Lorelei raises her head. 'But why not, Grand Counselor?'

"This catches the red-haired woman by surprise. It is clear for all

to see that she is not used to one of her subjects questioning her

decision. 'Did I hear you correctly Lorelei? How dare you question my

decision? Just who do you think you are?'

"Lorelei stands her ground even though Andrea remains in the blazing bonfire that roars between her and the Grand Counselor. 'We are a democracy. We all have a say in the decisions that we as a people make. I would not arbitrarily question a decision that is made upon due consideration, but there has been no debate. There has been no asking our sisters if they have an opinion on this subject. It is a question that needs to be asked. Are we just narcissistic women who care only about ourselves and our matriarchic society? What we always thought was good about what we created is that we are truly a sisterhood. A sisterhood is caring. We care about each other as women. We care about each other as mothers. We care about each other's children as an extended family. We even care about the men in our lives, if only to keep them subjugated and servile. But underneath it all we are caring individuals. How can we turn our backs on children in pain, children who suffer from disease and trauma? Above and beyond our Lotus ethic, we are caring individuals. I for one think we should give our Lotus blossoms to the children who need them much more than we do.'

"Now the red-haired woman becomes afraid. An idea has penetrated her world she is not prepared to stop. It sticks like a dagger into the very heart of her power and the grand concepts that enable her

242

power. She does not have a good idea of how to respond since Lorelei

was the other woman to receive votes from her sisters to be the Grand

Counselor. She has to take her ideas seriously. But maybe this is the

opportunity to get rid of her once and for all. 'Who among you would

destroy all we have built? Who amongst you besides Lorelei?' she asks.

"The apparitions emerge from the shadows, first as white faces

and then as black shrouded figures, each with long flowing black hair.

At first they don't indicate a response to the red-haired woman's

question. But then one hand goes up. That woman looks around

defiantly as the red-haired woman stonily watches to see what will

happen. Then another hand goes up. Slowly all of the hands come up,

one at a time to indicate agreement.

"The Grand Counselor cannot believe what she sees. It is the

voluntary destruction of the Lotus Eaters, fed by their own

humaneness. The red-haired woman had not seen that a conflict of such

core values could be resolved in favor of the larger more general society

at the expense of their own unique culture. Lorelei silently crosses the

courtyard and ascends the throne as the red-haired former Grand

Counselor steps aside. 'Sisters. We have spoken. From the bottom of my

heart I thank you for the courage to do what is right. We must devise a plan to provide our Lotus blossoms to the neediest of sick children.

Mister bear, would you help us with this task? Once it is complete then

we will send you back to the Supreme Bear Council with our pledge of

aid.'

"Ralph enjoys the next week as the guest of the Lotus Eaters,

helping them to make their plans. It is during this week that Ralph

discovers the secret of the sunset. All of the men are nocturnal, which is

to say they sleep during the day and work through the night. They

learned this behavior in college. They have not adjusted, since they have

become dependent upon the Lotus blossom euphoria. The Lotus

blossom removes all aggression, but energizes their work. The men are

very productive all night long. That is when they hunt. All of the

animals in the dark forest know they are fair game once the sun sets.

Thus, the animals will attack other animals if they believe they are being

hunted. For that reason the women all stay home at night while the

men conduct the hunt.

"And thus Ralph spends his week making new friends and

learning about how a different society grew. He learns how, now that

the enabler of that society was about to be diverted for a larger purpose,

the Lotus Eaters intend to manage the change that results. Ralph isn't sure their plans will work out quite the way they hope. But he is happy

the sick children soon will have the benefit of the Lotus blossoms to

ease their pain and help with their adjustments. Soon he will return

home to his mother and father. He will present the plan of the Lotus

Eaters to the Supreme Bear Council. Even the Master of Ordeals will

recognize that Ralph is close to completing his ordeals and having a

little girl of his own.

"But before that, he has to return through the deep dark forest. He

must hold on for dear life. He will pray that whoever leads him out will

not loosen their grip. If that should happen, Ralph will never again be

seen or heard from."

"No. He has to return to me. After all he's been through?" SJ

almost cries.

Dr. Hamilton smiles at SJ, but continues on. "Anyway, Lorelei

picks up Ralph and raises him onto her shoulders. She tells him to hold

on tightly for they will be traveling very fast. If he falls off he will most

certainly die. Ralph does as he is told, although the only thing he can

hold onto is her hair. He wraps it around his paws and leans down on

her head as she moves into the dark and mysterious woods.

"Ralph soon cannot see. It seems as if Lorelei travels faster and faster. She leans left and right. Ralph hears the wind in his ears and the sounds of the whooshing by trees and other impediments in their path. Lorelei sees all and knows where she goes, avoiding obstacles that Ralph can only guess at.

"She makes a particularly sharp move to her left. One of Ralph's hands comes loose. He falls off her shoulders, but hangs on with his one good paw, dangling below her face and looking up into her glowing eyes.

"Lorelei discovers him. Hoists him back up onto her shoulders without slowing or breaking her stride. Ralph grasps her hair with his other paw. He settles into place, hunkering down once more hoping to flow across the path with her.

"Soon the darkness begins to lift. Ralph sees a clearing up ahead with light coming down amongst the tall trees. Lorelei slows. In only a moment she walks into the clearing as if she had been strolling through the trees. Ralph knows that was far from the case.

"Ralph jumps down and looks back up at Lorelei. 'How can I thank you for all you have done and all you are about to do?'

"It is I who should thank you, Ralph the Bear. We have been blind to the world around us. Content to live a sheltered and self-absorbed existence. You have helped us see once more that we have an obligation to be citizens of the world. We will share the secrets we have discovered for the benefit of all mankind."

"And bear-kind." Ralph reminds her.

"She shakes his paw and displays a generous smile, 'And bear-kind.' In a moment she is gone, once more traversing the dark path between the world of light and the village of dark. Ralph smiles in remembrance of his harrowing journey. He begins the long walk home with a whistle and a smile."

Genevieve had a busy day at work and is tired when she reaches the hospital. When she enters the hospital room, the pirate formerly known as SJ sits on her bed in her pajamas, patch over her right eye and with most of her hair now missing. SJ waits patiently for her. SJ moves over to get up, but slides off the bed and collapses to the floor. Genevieve keeps walking towards her expecting she will pick herself up, but she does not.

"Momma, help me up." The cry precedes the raised arms. Genevieve drops her things and races to her daughter.

"What is it baby?"

"I don't know Momma."

Genevieve picks her up and carries her out to the nurse's station. The same nurse comes out, "Please call Doctor Hamilton. She can't stand." Genevieve hugs her baby.

"Momma, you're hugging too tight."

"I'm sorry, baby." Tears stream down her face and she doesn't know what to do or where to go so she continues to stand in front of the nurse's station.

"He's on his way." The nurse tells her, hanging up the phone.

"Momma, I'm scared. Why don't my legs work?"

"We'll just have to ask Doctor Hamilton that question now, won't we?"

The nurse comes around and touches Genevieve on the arm, "Why don't we go back to your room?" Genevieve doesn't move, absorbed with SJ. The nurse puts gentle pressure on her arm to get her attention.

"What?"

"Your room?" The nurse nods toward her room.

When Dr. Hamilton arrives, Genevieve sits on the bed still holding SJ, rocking her back and forth. He can see her fear and her tear-stained face. Curiously SJ doesn't have the same look, but seems to be more puzzled than frightened.

He holds out his arms and takes the child from her mother. Genevieve rises and Dr. Hamilton lies her down on her back in her bed.

He stretches out her legs, one at a time and then flexes each one, gently twisting and turning them, watching her eye as he does so. "Can you feel anything when I do this, Miss Pirate?"

SJ shakes her head.

"How about this?"

SJ shakes her head again.

He picks her up and rests her against him while he talks to her mother. "I'm going to walk her though a couple of tests so I can see what's going on."

"How long will it take?"

"Couple hours, but I'll stay with her through them."

"I'm sure you have other patients."

"I do, but they're all being well taken care of."

It was almost as if he could read her mind and Genevieve gratefully smiles back at him.

Almost to the minute, two hours later Dr. Hamilton and an orderly bring SJ back on a gurney. SJ sleeps, exhausted from the needles and the tests. Once in the room, the orderly lifts the sleeping girl off the gurney and places her gently into the bed and tucks her in.

Dr. Hamilton motions for Genevieve to follow him out into the hall. Once they are outside he speaks to her, "She'll be fine. Let's go down to the cafeteria. Have you eaten?"

Genevieve shakes her head but follows him almost as if on autopilot.

When they enter the cafeteria most of the food lines are closed so he picks up an apple and a cup of coffee. She just takes an apple and he pays for both. They go to a table and sit across from each other, but she won't look into his eyes.

"The mass of the tumor has shifted. She can see out of both eyes again, but now it impinges on her motor receptors, causing interference. That's the bad news, now the good news is the experimental drug seems to have slowed things down. I think there's a good chance that she'll be able to walk again soon, if the drugs continue to work and her brain compensates. But that's a big if. We have to keep our fingers and toes crossed on this one."

"The drugs seem to be working?" She can't believe her ears.

"That's what the MRI suggests. Now listen to me carefully. The drugs seem to have slowed things down; I did not say they shrank the tumor. In fact it still grows, only much slower than before. That's allowing her brain to make adjustments. That's why her vision returned. Hopefully her motor skills will too. But the objective has been to shrink the tumor so Dr. Grant can remove it."

"We're still talking the surgical option?" Genevieve hasn't really thought about surgery, hoping Dr. Hamilton could do something to prevent that course of action.

"The only other option has always been that the medication completely kills the tumor, but that rarely happens in these cases."

"And the surgery is her best chance for a cure?" The weariness evident in her voice even to herself.

"I think so. I'm encouraged the growth has slowed, but that's not enough. I hoped this treatment would shrink the tumor. It hasn't yet. So

I want to add another course of treatment to improve our chances. We have to shrink the tumor so Dr. Grant can safely remove it without affecting anything else." Dr. Hamilton rubs his face with his hand and then takes a bite from the apple.

This frustrates Genevieve. She wants answers. "Why does it seem that every time we talk about this we're always talking about probabilities? It's seems like we really don't know anything and everything is a guess."

"I could tell you someone will live ten years. The reality is that it is only a guess because there are so many factors at work that predicting with any kind of accuracy is impossible, particularly the longer you project into the future. You know I could see a patient who has Leukemia. All my tests may tell me that person will live a year. Five minutes after they walk out of my office they are run over by a bus and killed. All my science says the person will live a year, but my guess was off by almost a year. Do you see what I mean?"

"It's all so ... scary, how little we seem to know." She observes dismally and goes quiet.

He waits respectfully, chewing on his apple interrupted by an occasional sip of his coffee. Then he asks, "Can I change the topic on you?"

"I really wish you would."

"What are we going to do about Bearmas?"

She looks at him as if he were crazy.

"I think it's time she got her bear." He continues.

"But I can't afford to buy her one right now." She sinks into that same overwhelmed state again.

"I think that's the Supreme Bear Council's problem, not yours."

She gives him a puzzled look.

Ralph's Bearmas

The next day the orderly comes for SJ early to start the additional course of therapy. Genevieve spent the night and she hurries off to work early because she intends to come back during her lunch hour.

She rushes through the morning, gathering facts and data as fast as she can so she is able to prepare her claim summaries. And then the clock inches toward noon. She bolts out the door to find out how the new treatment has affected SJ.

If only they weren't so expensive.

Genevieve finds SJ on a gurney in the hallway next to the nurse's station talking with Dr. Hamilton. The nurses busily run in and out of SJ's room. Finally one nurse comes out and proclaims, "We're ready."

Dr. Hamilton nods for Genevieve to come help him push SJ into her room.

She kisses SJ on her nearly bald and now eye patchless head. "Hi, honey."

Together Dr. Hamilton and Genevieve push SJ into her room to find balloons and streamers hung from the ceiling and a big sign proclaiming: MERRY BEARMAS. The nurses, aides and housekeepers await them in the room. Jacob is there as well, in his wheelchair, looking puzzled as he inspects the decorations. Everyone claps their hands as SJ comes in.

The orderly with Dr. Hamilton's assistance slides SJ into her bed and arranges pillows so she can sit up by herself. Dr. Hamilton then raises his hand for quiet. "Does anyone know the story of Bearmas?"

SJ pipes up, "I do."

"I don't, but I'm eager to hear it." Jacob adds.

Dr. Hamilton asks, "But do you mind if I tell it to everyone?"

SJ nods okay.

"Well Bearmas is the celebration of the birth of a bear. Did you
know that when little girls and boys are sick or alone and frightened
that somewhere in the world a bear is born who is destined to be theirs
and theirs alone?" Dr. Hamilton turns to look at SJ, letting everyone
know who the recipient will be and to make sure he has her approval,
that he has the story right.

"Now that bear has to prove to its parents and the Supreme Bear
Council it is a worthy bear, worthy of being the one special bear for a
little boy or girl. The bear has to undergo a series of ordeals where, if it
succeeds, it becomes worthy. But if the bear fails even one of the
ordeals, the bear becomes disgraced and must join the salmon hunters,
the group of redeeming bears. These bears must fish the most remote
rivers of Alaska for a year, feeding all of the northern bear tribes. At the
end of the year the redeeming bear must join the baklava bakers, where
he or she gathers nuts and honey and makes baklava for all of the
northern bear tribes. After a year making baklava the bear has
redeemed himself and become eligible to again challenge the ordeals for
his or her chosen boy or girl. But this is the last chance. If the redeemed
bear successfully makes it through the ordeals, the bear comes and lives
with the chosen boy or girl. But if the bear fails at even one ordeal, it is
cast out of the bear tribes and must wander the wilderness of the most
far northern reaches of Alaska."

Another visual check with SJ, who nods to him and he keeps
going. "And that's why sometimes boys and girls get small bears;
they're the ones who are successful with the ordeals the first time
through. If a much larger bear arrives, then you know that bear didn't
make it through the first time, but is a redeemed bear. Redeemed bears

have many more stories to tell and are also good salmon fishermen and baklava bakers. And that's why when we celebrate Bearmas, we always eat salmon and baklava in remembrance of the redeeming bears."

Dr. Hamilton and Genevieve both wish SJ, "Merry Bearmas."

SJ asks, "Do I get the bear in the attic?"

Genevieve shakes her head, "No, SJ. That bear belonged to your Aunt Yvette. You never met her because she died when she was about ten years old, long before you were born.

SJ seems curious about this, never having heard this particular story before, but she says nothing more.

"Now, Bearmas is not the bear's birthday, but the celebration of the bear's birthday and the completion of the ordeals that bring the bear to a little girl or boy. The attic bear was loved by your Aunt Yvette. Another bear was born to love and be loved by just you and do you know who that bear is?"

SJ gets wide-eyed as a nurse brings in a big brown bear, nearly as big as SJ.

"Is this Ralph?" She asks awe struck by how big he is.

"Yes." Dr. Hamilton tells her.

"Can he fish for salmon and make baklava?" SJ asks him, at which cue the nutritionist wheels in a cart with salmon, juice and baklava. The rest of the nurses come in for the celebration and join them in their Bearmas feast. One of the nurses brings in a small radio playing music. The nurses dance while SJ laughs at their uncoordinated efforts. The nurses drag Genevieve and Dr. Hamilton to their feet to join in the dancing. Soon the room is full of dancing nurses, all moving in an awfully uncoordinated fashion to rock and roll music.

A slow song starts on the radio. Everyone sits down, although

THE FIRST BEARMAS

Genevieve and Dr. Hamilton linger behind the nurses.

The salmon and baklava have disappeared, only a little juice remains. The orderly wheels a sleeping Jacob out as the nurse carries the radio back to her station.

SJ's head keeps bobbing as she leans against Ralph.

Genevieve smiles at Dr. Hamilton. "This has to be the best Bearmas ever. I really have to thank you and everyone. I couldn't have done this."

"Thank the Supreme Bear Council. They chose Ralph. This is just a traditional Bearmas feast." Dr. Hamilton tells her.

"But what about the other ordeal?" realizing she has to get back to work.

"I thought we could just have Ralph tell it to her, after all he experienced it."

"He'll need an interpreter." SJ notes.

Genevieve accepts that with a nod. She tucks in SJ who keeps her arm partially around Ralph, and kisses her daughter's nearly bald head.

Late that night, Genevieve creeps down the hospital hall toward SJ's room. As she passes the nurses station she is surprised to find Dr.

255

Hamilton there filling out paperwork on the computer.

"Hi, there." He looks at his watch and realizes how late it really is. "Later than usual for you?"

"Well you know, Bearmas put me a little behind on my work. I can't afford to lose my job."

"I remember." He looks back at the screen.

"I wanted to thank you properly for everything you and the staff did here for Bearmas. SJ will never forget it, I'll never forget it. I was amazed you remembered the story so well."

"I had a good teacher." His warm and genuine smile warms her too.

"You know that's the happiest I've seen her since everything began. And it's all because of you."

"I only elaborated on what you started. So let's stop singing each other's praises and just be happy we have her for another day." He concludes, but then remembers, "Her father. She said he's dead. Is that true?"

Genevieve would rather not go into this right now, but she owes him so much she nods and puts down the things she carries. "Yes... with the Army. A training accident."

"You never married, but you obviously loved him. You have his child."

"I doubt I ever loved him. I was pregnant at sixteen, dropped out of school in my junior year to have her. Never went back because the son-of-a-bitch never acknowledged her."

"That was his loss. She's a tremendous kid."

"Luckily she doesn't take after him."

256

"I can see who she does take after and it's not your mother. Although she may have some of her sense of humor." Genevieve is uncomfortable with his appreciative look. It makes her feel good and yet she doesn't feel worthy of it.

"Why didn't you finish school?"

Genevieve tries to control her anger, "By the time I had her, my father had left my mother to hook up with another woman. SJ's father ran off to play soldier boy and get himself killed. I was all she had. She's my baby."

"That still doesn't answer my question."

"It was just too hard. With learning a job and then making sure I was good at it. Trying to be home with her as much as I could, there was only room for two priorities in my life."

"And that's why no boyfriends since?"

She can't look at him now, this is getting way too uncomfortable. But somehow it feels good to have someone like him appreciate her. "I guess."

She looks towards SJ's room for a long moment, and then remembers, "But I did pick this up this week." She shows him the General Educational Development study guide for her high school equivalency exam. "I've signed up to take the test in a couple of weeks. I thought studying might help me get my mind off things. Also fulfill a promise I made to her a long time ago."

"Which was?"

"To stop using my current situation as an excuse. I need to make something more of myself. I can be as stubborn as a mule at times. I always want to do it my way. But I know I can be a lot more than I am right now. This may only be a first step. It may take me ten years or more to get a degree, but I will do it."

"I know you will. I've only met a few people in my life as determined as you." His tone is respectful and hints at more than mere appreciation.

They look at each other across the nurse's station counter. It's an awkward moment. Neither seems to know what to say to conclude this frank and intimate discussion.

The night nurse comes back from her rounds and sees them there. She goes into the bathroom, giving them a minute to say good night.

"Well, the morning will be here soon. I have another long day ahead of me if I intend to keep my job." Very nervous and at the same time probably overly cautious, she finally thinks how to conclude what she doesn't want to conclude, "Thank you again for everything. Good night."

Dr. Hamilton looks sad, nods at some private thought, and then adds his, "Good night. Sleep well."

"Yeah, really on that chair." She laughs, picks up her things and goes to join SJ.

The next evening Genevieve finishes a little earlier at work. She rushes to the hospital to see SJ before she goes to sleep. The Merry Bearmas decorations remain. She finds SJ sitting up in bed, talking with Ralph and one of the nurses.

"Hi, kiddo. How's Ralph?" Genevieve asks as she comes over to give her daughter a hug and kiss, which she does. The nurse gets up to leave, but Genevieve motions for her to stay as she puts her things down.

The nurse comments, "SJ has been telling me the story of Ralph's ordeals. She says he had more but Ralph hasn't had time to tell her what they are yet. But we're all sure looking forward to hearing those stories, when you're ready."

"Sounds like you and Ralph have had a very good day." Genevieve concludes.

"They have. This has been a very good un-Bearmas day, or is it a Post Bearmas celebration? I forget." The nurse turns to SJ looking for help.

"It's a un-Bearmas day." SJ informs them.

"Well you have a merry un-Bearmas day, then," The nurse smiles at SJ as she leaves the room.

"And a very merry un-Bearmas day to you, nurse." SJ says in return.

Genevieve sits down next to SJ and Ralph. "You look much better today than yesterday, even though yesterday was Bearmas."

"I'll bet it was the salmon and baklava. Did you know Ralph caught the salmon and made the baklava for us?"

Genevieve wonders if the nurse told her this or if SJ decided it happened this way. "No, I didn't know. Did Ralph tell you that?"

"No, Doctor Hamilton did. I really like him. You should keep him."

"I should what?" The comment catches Genevieve off guard.

"Keep him. He could be my daddy." SJ has clearly been thinking about this.

"Why would you want him to be your daddy? You hardly know him." Genevieve wonders if he said something to SJ about her.

"He knows about bear ordeals. It seems most people don't."

"Why do you say that?"

"Well the nurse didn't know, but Ralph has been filling her in."

"Oh, I see. That can be something you and Ralph make your special mission in life, to let people know about Bearmas."

"And un-Bearmas days, so people will greet each other with a Merry Un-Bearmas to you."

"This sounds vaguely like a story I read to you a long time ago."

"Like un-Birthdays?" SJ admits.

"Yeah. Are you sure you're not getting things confused here?"

"Well, I like the sound of it anyway." SJ gives ground but doesn't give up.

"So what are you and Ralph doing tonight? I have to study for a little while."

SJ looks at the GED book and consults with Ralph telepathically. "Ralph wants to study with you. He said he never got his high school diploma either. So he wants to learn all that stuff too."

Genevieve kisses SJ on the top of her head and gives Ralph a squeeze. "Good. It's always better to study with someone than to study alone. Okay, let's take a look at the first lesson here. World history. First question. What color was George Washington's white horse?"

SJ looks at her mother quizzically.

"Can Ralph answer that question for me?" SJ asks Genevieve. She puts her head to Ralph as if listening. "Ralph says it must be white." SJ answers for her bear.

"That's correct. Ralph must have studied for a long time to learn all that history."

"So do you have a question for me?" SJ asks.

"Sure. Let's do science."

"Okay, I like science." SJ responds.

"What common food does the honey bee make? You can ask Ralph if you like because I think he might know."

SJ puts her head to Ralph's and talks with him telepathically. And a moment later she has her answer. "Ralph says the honey bee contributes to baklava." And SJ starts laughing.

Genevieve pats Ralph on the head, "Thank you very much Ralph. I think it's time your partner in crime and you get some sleep. You have a lot of work to do to get well. Now that Ralph is here to help you, I know you'll both do a splendid job of just that."

"Bathroom first." SJ reminds her mother.

Genevieve picks up her daughter and carries her into the bathroom where they prepare for bed. A few minutes later she carries the washed-up and tooth-brushed ex-pirate formerly known as SJ back to her bed. She tucks SJ into her un-Bearmas bed for the night. She turns down all the lights except the one over the chair. Genevieve kisses both her daughter and her daughter's one and only bear, good night.

SJ wraps her arm around Ralph as best she can and closes her eyes.

Genevieve sits down in the chair, picks up the GED study guide and starts the long trip to getting her college degree. After only a few minutes she looks over. SJ has fallen fast asleep. But Ralph remains ever alert, making sure no further harm comes to his best friend in the whole world.

Genevieve lets her mind wander for a few minutes, back to SJ's question about Dr. Hamilton being her father. She has to admit she is attracted to him. That exact thought had occurred to her. She also remembers how SJ pointed out the sadness in his eyes. That bothers her. It also makes her afraid she could not help him cope with the sadness that must come with being a doctor when some of your patients don't get better. But at least SJ feels better today. As he said last night, let's be glad we have her for one more day. *One more day. Tomorrow is another day. Maybe there's something to this.*

The next day Genevieve works through her client list, but when she finishes her calls at one-thirty, she forwards her phone to voicemail. She reaches into her lower desk drawer and removes the GED study guide, and an apple she bought at the hospital cafeteria. She takes both items with her and walks out to a small courtyard in the center of the office building, where, although warm, she can soak up sunshine while she also soaks up the information she will need to know for the test.

The warmth helps her to relax. The air conditioning chill she feels each day oozes out of her body. Soon she feels less on edge. She reads the material, answers the questions on a legal pad and then checks her answers at the end of each chapter. She hasn't found the question about George Washington's white horse, but she would not be surprised if she did. What amazes her is how much of the history, English and science she does know. It's the math part she struggles with. Although she was always a good math student before, she doesn't have a need for calculus in the work she does. So she hasn't used higher math and in some cases never learned it.

She takes a bite of her big red apple. She reflects for a moment about math. She is a reader, and she always reads to SJ, sometimes things her mother thinks are inappropriate for a seven year old. But everything she reads is a classic in one sense or another. But even she was surprised about how real the dream about the Gestapo taking away

262

the bear in the attic was to SJ. It just never occurred to her she would translate the story that way. But she remains glad she shares her love of literature with her little girl. She asks questions most seven year olds would never think of. She seems to have a very good memory, bringing up things they read about long afterward.

All of this gives her confidence she will pass the test if she just gets through the math section. She determines she must spend the most time reviewing math. She takes another big bite of the apple. Dean comes out into the courtyard. She tries to remember if she has ever seen him out here before. But then she usually works through lunch. It has been a long time since she has been out here as well.

"Hey. I went looking for you. Janie said she saw you head this way. What's up?" he asks as he approaches her bench.

"I decided to take a lunch hour."

"New Year's resolution?" He wants to know the reason, since she almost never takes one and stays in.

"No … well maybe. I'm studying."

"For what?"

She hesitates, not sure if she wants him to know, because she intended to just bring in the certificate after she takes the exam and hand it to him. She knows in the back of her mind she saw that as an opportunity not to set anyone's expectations in case she should fail the exam. But now, she realizes, she should tell him. Not discussing what was going on with SJ had nearly cost her the job. She has had to work a lot harder since to keep him happy.

She closes the cover to her study guide and lets him read it.

"GED? Well … it's about time. Didn't I talk to you about taking that what … almost seven years ago? You know you'll get an automatic raise if you pass it. Not much of a raise because of how long you've been here, but still money in your pocket."

She had forgotten about the raise. It actually would have been substantial if she had taken the test when she first joined the company. As a new mother she was still adjusting to life with a new borne and learning the job. Back then time with SJ was more important than anything else. But now, she realizes she is taking the first tentative step towards the life she knows she deserves but hasn't allowed herself to obtain, always thinking it should just happen. She bought the book when she should have, would have, spent that money on a bear for SJ before. It worked out because Ralph is a much nicer and much bigger bear than she could have ever afforded. But still she feels guilty about doing something for herself at the expense of something her daughter wanted. And now she sees Ralph really is something SJ needs.

"So when are you taking the test?" Dean asks interrupting her thoughts.

"Oh, couple of weeks. Already signed up for it. You know me, got to have a deadline to keep me motivated."

"So soon? Are you going to be ready that quickly?"

She considers his question because she was having the same doubts when she picked the date. Now that she's part way into the study guide the only part that concerns her is the math.

"Yeah, I think so. You know I've always read a lot. I think that helps."

Dean nods in understanding. "Well anyway, I think it's great you're doing this. I wanted to tell you I'm pleased you've gotten back on track. But your performance rating is going to really suffer this time. I wanted to talk to you about it."

She knows her performance rating is generally derived from the statistics they keep on everyone. Her statistics have always been at the highest, particularly for customer satisfaction, cycle time from claim filing to check issuance, and settlement percentage of initial claim value. She realizes in the last several weeks all of those statistics have fallen to the bottom of the department, but she knows her performance has really come back up in the last few days. Her time with SJ has suffered as a result. If she hadn't taken those four days off and rested she may have recovered on her statistics faster, but then again she may never have gotten the rest she needed to catch up as she has. *But still a few weeks out of seven years and now he's telling me my performance for the year is going to take a hit. This really sucks.*

"I don't know if we've talked about how the performance rating system works, but we're at the end of a quarter. The end of the quarter is weighted heavier than the rest of the year." He dives right in to the discussion.

She didn't know that because her performance was always so consistent she never saw much variation in the overall scores.

"And we also weight the fourth quarter heavier than the first three. So there's good news and bad news here for you. First, you're going to take a hit this quarter no matter how much you've improved this week. You couldn't have picked a worse time in the quarter to have this happen. That's water over the dam at this point. You have been the highest rated member of the team for as long as I've been your supervisor. That's not going to be the case for this month or for the quarter. You still have a chance to bring your year performance rating back up, but I took a look at that. Even if you get back to your old level of performance for the rest of the year, this quarter will knock you out of the top spot. And that means you won't get the bonus that goes with the number one rating. You know that's a pretty substantial bonus even at your salary level."

Genevieve hasn't thought about the bonus. It's what she always uses to pay for SJ's Christmas presents and catch up on the bills she just never seems to keep paid. What he has just told her is there will be no Christmas this year for SJ.

"How much is the raise for the High School Equivalency? Is it close to the value of the bonus?" She tries to calculate how she will be able to stay afloat.

"I don't know what it will be for you now. I'll have to go look and let you know."

"Would you? That'll be important."

"It must be tough trying to support SJ and yourself on what you make here."

"You don't know the half of it." The comment slips out before she censors herself. She instantly regrets it. She watches his reaction and it seems to be accepting, rather than critical. She breathes a sigh of relief. "Please don't misunderstand me; I'm grateful for the job and your support and help. But yes, I don't have even an extra nickel to spend. Unplanned expenses set me back until that bonus each year, when I generally get myself caught up again. That's why the raise will be so important."

"Let me look at that when I go back in and I'll send you an email with the amount based on your current salary." He looks at his watch, "Oops, I've taken up most of your lunch hour and kept you from studying."

"I need to get my customer sat rating back up." She shares this with him to indicate she has gotten the message about performance loud and clear. She follows him back to the door. He opens and holds it for her, then follows her inside.

That evening when Genevieve reaches the hospital, the night nurse stops her in the hall and tells her that Dr. Hamilton wanted to go over the latest test results with her in his office. As usual, he's working late so she can go over now if she would.

Genevieve tells the nurse she will as soon as she has seen SJ.

She enters the Merry Bearmas room and finds SJ sitting up with Ralph, reading a book together. The first impression she has with Ralph's distant stare is the bear pictures the story SJ tells him. She has seen that look on SJ when she reads about strange and wonderful places that neither of them have ever seen or probably will ever see.

"Hi, kiddo. How's today?" Genevieve shudders, finding the hospital room cooler than usual, or maybe it is just that she hasn't warmed up from outside yet.

"Merry un-Bearmas to you, too." A cheerful response comes from SJ.

"Merry un-Bearmas." She comes to the bed, kisses the top of her daughter's nearly bald head and gives her a hug.

"Where's Ralph's hug and kisses? He gets very upset when people pay attention to me but ignore him. He has feelings too, you know." The very adult-like response from SJ causes Genevieve to think about her behavior for a moment. She's always been very adult-like except when her feelings are hurt or she's feeling lonely or unsure of something. Then the Momma plead gets attached. Today there's no Momma plead. But then again, she's not sure if that's a good thing or not.

She hugs both Ralph and SJ together eliciting a protest from SJ, "Ralph needs his own hugs, not shared hugs!" So Genevieve picks up Ralph and gives him his is very own hug and a kiss on the top of his head too. She then returns the bear to the protective confines of SJ's embrace.

"You okay for a bit if I go see Doctor Hamilton?"

SJ looks up curiously at her mother and considers the request.

"It's not a date if that's what you're thinking. He wants to show me some of your test results." She watches as her daughter's expectation changes to remembrances of tests and needles. "I'll be right back."

"No you won't. You'll be a long time and by the time you get back, I'll be asleep, Momma."

She hears the Momma plead and her heart falls. "No, I'll be back before you go to sleep. Promise."

"You need to study math tonight." SJ reminds her mother.

Genevieve nods, "Thanks for reminding me. I'd forgotten," even though she has not, but she plans to work the problems after SJ goes to sleep.

She literally races across the cold and blustery square to the office building. She has no problem finding Dr. Hamilton's office as it is the only one with lights on within that corridor. She opens the door and calls, "Doctor Hamilton? It's Genevieve Wilcox."

"In my office." The reply comes from down the hallway.

A moment later she peeks into his office. He looks at MRI images on a wall mounted screen next to his desk. "That SJ?"

"Merry un-Bearmas to you and if you're referring to the ex-pirate formerly known as SJ … yes." Dr. Hamilton replies.

"Merry un-Bearmas. I see you've had your dose of my daughter for the day." The tone is light and a smile tries to occupy her face. But she is not sure if she wants it to succeed or not. He looks up at her and she can see an appreciation for her in his eyes, which always warms her.

"Always a pleasure to have my daily dose. I wanted you to see something because it is good news and I know you need all of that you can get," he begins. "Look here." He points to two side-by-side images of SJ's brain. "The one on the left is last Wednesday, two days after we started the experimental treatment. The one on the right is this afternoon. She's very good about all the tests, by the way, but she really doesn't like them."

"I don't like tests much myself." She's thinking of a different kind of test.

"In this image you can see where the tumor has spread into these areas. Looking at the earlier images we can see where it applies pressure and why her motor control has been affected. But in today's image, it appears to have receded, particularly from those new areas. I think she'll be able to walk soon, if she can't now."

Relieved and hopeful, Genevieve responds, "Thank you. Thank you so much."

"Now don't get too excited about all this. The tumor mass has receded from some areas, but not as much or as fast as I'd hoped."

The hope in Genevieve's eyes flickers. "What do you think's happening?"

"Like we talked about, it's all a guess because we don't know enough yet. Several scenarios, but I think the two most likely are the treatment is working and it will continue to retreat and shrink the mass. That's what my literary friends call the Rosy Scenario." He lets her think about the first scenario for a moment before he continues, "And on the other hand it could mean that the treatment isn't as effective as we need. Now my business friends would call that the worst case scenario."

Genevieve's heart can't take much more of this roller coaster ride and she has to sit down. "What do we do?"

He points to the new image. "If it continues to shrink but stops at some point, then would be the right time to remove it."

"Surgery." She doesn't know if this is a good thing or not. She doesn't want to see her baby cut knowing surgery always results in unforeseen complications. It could change her personality, or leave her without certain brain functions or memories or who knows what? But it could save her life. Right now that's all Genevieve wants.

"Surgery is always the least preferred solution. But in this case it's only a matter of when, not if." He concludes the thought.

"So if the Rosy Scenario plays out you think it will only be a temporary improvement?"

"This is a particularly aggressive disease, Genevieve. The experimental treatment is so new we don't have any data about long term effects."

He called her Genevieve. That's the first time. She didn't even hear the rest of what he said. *Has he crossed some bridge? What does that mean?* This puts her in an even greater turmoil than before. She notices his looks and feels her own reactions to them. Now she sees one more sign of what? Growing affection for her? Or is it just collegial respect? What is he trying to say to her? She has to put this aside and find out what he said. "Could you repeat that last statement, I'm sorry, there's just so much to absorb here." She tries the best excuse she can think of.

He smiles at her with that knowing smile. *Can he actually read my mind?*

"The experimental drug is so new we don't have any data about long term effects. So the answer to your question is we just don't know if it would be better."

"What do you recommend?" This seems to be the logical question now.

"We wait and watch it carefully."

"So should I be more hopeful?" She asks, almost afraid to be.

"I am."

She looks at the wall clock in his office and rises abruptly, "I told her I'd only be a minute. I get so little time with her…"

He rises as well, "I understand. Good night."

She sees that same look in his eyes, *if only I understood what it means*. She was never very good at understanding what men think. If she was, she probably never would have gone to bed with a man, no, a boy - at sixteen - that she hardly knew. But then again, she never would have had SJ.

She nods, finally, "Thanks for everything, especially giving us hope. Good night." She thinks she sees the sadness return in his eyes. *What does that mean? But SJ's waiting. It probably has nothing to do with me.*

She leaves his office and hurries back to SJ.

The next morning Genevieve gets ready for work in the hospital room bathroom. SJ stirs in bed moving about more than Genevieve had noticed over the last few days. *A good sign*, she thinks.

SJ yawns, pats Ralph on the head, "Wake up sleepy head." She looks around and sees her mother in the bathroom. "You're still here?"

"It's early for you, only about six."

"Merry un-Bearmas."

"And a particularly Merry un-Bearmas to you my dear," Genevieve wants to be upbeat. "How do you feel?"

"The spots are gone."

"The black spots you were seeing?" She asks SJ to make sure they are talking about the same thing.

"Yes. I don't see any spots. Thank you, Mister Ralph. Did you take away my spots?"

"I believe he did." Genevieve wants her to think Ralph helps her, because if she believes he does, Ralph, Bearmas and Doctor Hamilton have all conspired to help her little girl. "Thank you, Mister Ralph."

Genevieve finishes pinning her hair into place. One last check on her blemishes. She flies to the bed, gives SJ a big hug and kisses, picks up Ralph and does the same. "Do you want me to help you sit up before I go, or will you go back to sleep?"

"Let me try, Momma."

She realizes SJ is not sure she can do it, but she wants to try. So, Genevieve stands by ready to help if necessary.

SJ leans forward and pushes up with her arms. It's slow and she pushes hard, the strain shows in her face, but little by little she pushes herself up further and further until she can lean back against the headboard. "I did it, Momma!" SJ exclaims with excitement.

"Yes, you and Mister Ralph have another success for the day."

"I'm getting better. I can feel it, Momma."

"And I can see it too, kiddo." She kisses SJ once more. SJ puts her arms around her mother's neck to share the hug and the happiness she feels. "I'm going to work extra hard today so hopefully I can get here to see you earlier. Mister Ralph, you're in charge of making this ex-pirate, formerly known as SJ, get stronger yet. I want to see real improvement when I get back tonight."

"Yes, ma'am." SJ speaks for Ralph in a low voice that represents her thoughts of what a bear voice should sound like. "Momma, did Doctor Hamilton tell you I was getting better last night?"

"Yes. We talked about that. And see, you're better already."

"Will I be able to go home to Granma's soon?"

Genevieve hesitates and she sees the optimism in SJ melt away. "I hope so."

At work Genevieve shows Janie how to determine salvage values when she looks at the clock and sees that it's one-thirty. Time for study.

"Think you can do this now?" Genevieve asks Janie, who still works through the example in her mind.

"I think so, but let me do a couple more examples and if you'd check them for me?" Janie still works the problem in her mind as she answers.

"Sure, just bring them over." Genevieve opens her desk bottom drawer to retrieve the study guide and her now every day hospital apple for lunch. Janie stands up looking at the example, but notices the book as she turns away. "What are you reading?" Janie asks.

"Studying for a test." Genevieve admits although she had been hoping not to discuss it with Janie. Most everyone knows she never finished high school. But she hates to admit it to Janie, especially since she got her job because she has a degree.

"I'm a great test taker, maybe I can help you study." Janie's enthusiasm surprises Genevieve.

"This is probably way below you. And besides you've got your own things to learn for the job." She tries to think of more excuses but runs out.

"No, no. You've been teaching me, so this could be one way I can repay you. What is it?" Janie's smile and enthusiasm seems genuine to Genevieve. She's not sure what to do since she has been of the belief Janie was conspiring with Dean to get rid of her.

"It's the GED exam." She finally admits and drops the study guide on her desk.

Janie's surprise is real, *so she didn't know*, Genevieve realizes.

"Why…" Janie starts, but it takes her a minute to put it together. "You didn't graduate high school?"

"No."

"I never would have thought that. You're so smart and you know so much." Another moment goes by while more pieces fall together for Janie. "You ought to be able to ace this, no problem."

"I need help with the math. I never had calculus." Genevieve realizes she might be able to help after all.

"Calc is college level. Probably not more than a question or two on the test." Janie reasons.

"Are you good in math?" Genevieve fears the answer will be no.

"Aced every course in college. Let's walk though what's in the study guide and I'll explain anything you don't understand. How's that for a start?"

"That would be great. I'm taking the test next week, so I don't have much time."

Janie puts her hand on Genevieve's shoulder to reassure her. "We can probably cover everything you need to know there in an hour or two. Courtyard's a good place to study."

"So I've discovered. Before getting ready for this test I'd probably only been out there two or three times. Now it's becoming one of my favorite places."

Genevieve studies Janie's expression. She only sees helpfulness and concern. A great deal of confidence she has not seen before. But that makes sense. Taking tests is something Janie does well. Being able to help Genevieve appears to be something she really wants to do. *Maybe I misread her. Wouldn't be the first time I misread someone. Maybe Dean was right that we can be friends.* While Janice and Sandy had been helpful in her learning and doing her job, they had never been friends. Never done anything together outside of work. But then maybe she was never open to doing anything because she always wanted to get right home to SJ. *Maybe Janie will be a friend.*

That evening Genevieve returns from another long day at work, but she feels more positive than she has in a long time. SJ was better in the morning, even able to sit up without help. *Janie is going to be a godsend on the math.* They had gone through practically the whole study guide section on the math in a single lunch hour. Janie was right. There were only a few different study questions on calculus and Janie was easily able to explain what they wanted and how to do those problems. The rest she pretty much understood. And Janie had shown her some easier ways to do some of the problems. The doubts she had about passing the exam disappear. She knows she can pass this and probably even ace it, to use Janie's term. And best yet, she got through all her call backs early. She even left when everyone else did. *How many years has it been since I did that?*

As she comes down the hallway towards SJ's room she slows to greet the nurses. When she turns back towards SJ's room, she sees her little girl standing in the doorway waiting for her. She's holding the door jamb. Genevieve isn't sure if that's because she's not completely steady or she's just striking a pose for her.

"Momma, look!" SJ takes a step towards her and then another… and then walks normally, but doesn't run. Genevieve drops her things on the floor and kneels down to receive her hugs. Kisses follow and Genevieve is so happy.

She picks up her things and follows her daughter back into the room. "When were you able to walk again, SJ?" she asks. SJ consults Mister Ralph, "What time was it?" She listens to his telepathic response, "He says it was before lunch."

"Did you actually eat something today?

"They brought us salmon and baklava. Mister Ralph was a naughty bear because he ate all my baklava and I didn't get any." SJ gives Ralph a cross look.

"That's okay. The salmon is better for you anyway."

"We both ate all our salmon. It was almost as good as on Bearmas. Even Mister Ralph thought so." Genevieve changes out of her work clothes into her hospital sweats and tee shirt. She lets her hair down and washes off the make-up. When she steps out of the bathroom she finds Dr. Hamilton standing next to SJ, but looking in at her. Genevieve becomes instantly embarrassed.

"If I'd known you were coming by tonight I'd have…"

"You look great. I'm not a fancy guy, I take my women straight, don't I SJ?"

Genevieve comes out of the bathroom but leans back against the door jamb and waits to see what he has to say.

"I came by to see how our girl is doing. I had an early emergency this morning and didn't get by." Dr. Hamilton pats the bear on his head.

Genevieve anxiously looks at the door, "Well a friend is coming by to help me study in a few minutes. I could probably call her and ask her to come by later, except I don't have her number. She probably didn't go home from work either. I think she was going to the library to get some materials and come here."

Unfazed Dr. Hamilton presses on, "Not a problem, I'll only be a few minutes." Dr. Hamilton starts his examination, but seems to keep Genevieve in sight the whole time.

Janie shows up within a few minutes. Introduces herself to Dr. Hamilton, SJ, and Mister Ralph and as the nurses and housekeepers arrive, she meets them as well.

SJ tells the nurses and housekeepers there will be no ordeal tonight so they need to come back. When Dr. Hamilton finishes his examination he turns to Genevieve. "Nothing to worry about tonight."

"What does that mean?" Genevieve wants to know.

"It means nothing has changed since yesterday that is observable without more tests. I'd rather not put her through any more of them than I need to. I've been stretching her patience recently."

"I'd rather you stretch her imagination and challenge her than make everything simple because she's only seven." Genevieve wants Doctor Hamilton to not treat SJ as a little kid, because she never has.

"Yes, I understand you do that." The twinkle returns in his eye, "But I need to let you study, your friend is here and *Tempus Fugit*."

Janie approaches Dr. Hamilton remarks, "You seem really good with kids. How do you do that?" Genevieve doesn't like the look in Janie's eye, but she puts it aside, remembering she has no claim on the good doctor. He will have to look out for himself.

"I just like kids." His response sounds genuine.

"You must have a bunch of your own." Genevieve sees Janie

wants to test the waters.

"Never been married, but my patients are like an extended family."

"Wouldn't you like to have a houseful of your own to spoil and tell stories to?" All Genevieve can hear is Janie volunteering to pop those kids out for him one every nine months if he wants. She steps out into the hall and walks off the fear that Janie will win Dr. Hamilton's affections. She knows she would like nothing better than his affections for herself. But then she also knows she would be happy never to see him again if it meant SJ would live a normal life.

A few minutes later, Dr. Hamilton comes out with Janie. Genevieve remains very unsettled about Janie's interest in him, her gratitude to Janie for helping her study and everything else that continues to happen all at the same time.

That's the problem; it's all at the same time.

"I see she's walking. Her energy and feistiness seem to be returning."

"Thanks to your treatment."

"Don't underestimate the impact of what you've started here." He looks back at the room and then all around.

"What do you mean?" She's confused.

"Housekeepers coming to hear the ordeals and identifying with them. Look at SJ, how much she's improved since Bearmas. I don't know if it's the treatment or the bear, or if they need to go together. But any way you look at it, another day has passed. She's still with us, and she's happy and she's engaged. It's what I hope for with every one of my patients."

Genevieve knows he's right. She needs to be grateful for today.

Not look too far into the future, either expecting it to go back the way it was, or … to end up the other way. She brings herself back into the moment. She knows she should just be grateful. She leans forward and kisses him on the cheek. She then goes back to SJ and Janie.

Later Genevieve and Janie sit on the floor next to the bed. Janie explains one of the problems Genevieve got wrong, while SJ and Ralph sit on the bed watching from above like guardian angels.

"So then you simply solve the simultaneous equations to get the answer. The only thing tricky about it is getting it set up right. As long as you read the problem carefully you shouldn't have any issues." Janie concludes and shows her the calculation to get the right answer.

SJ asks Ralph a question, "Mister Ralph, did you understand how she did that problem? I think I'm going to need some help the next time I have to solve one."

Genevieve responds, "Don't worry, I'll help you with it."

"Why do I need to know how to solve problems like that?" SJ asks.

"It is part of the curriculum; everyone needs to know how to do it." Genevieve answers her.

"But I'm only seven. I won't need to know that for a long time. Maybe even a couple of weeks. I'm going to sleep and let you two old ladies gab all night."

"As long as Ralph understands it I guess you can." Genevieve smiles to Janie.

"Mister Ralph is a very smart bear, even though he didn't know what *Tempus Fugit* meant. I think he knows it now. Don't you Mister Ralph?" SJ tilts Ralph's head so it appears he nods in agreement.

"Okay, in the bathroom and get yourself ready for bed." Genevieve sounds tired. SJ climbs down and trundles into the bath as Genevieve concludes with Janie. "Thanks for staying later, it's been just incredibly helpful to me, particularly going through the ones I got wrong. You know you'd be a good math teacher,' Genevieve observes.

Janie reflects for a moment and then decides she can trust Genevieve. "You know that really is what I would rather be doing. Working with kids, helping them to learn."

"So why did you come to Richland?" Genevieve is confused.

"This is going to sound awful, but it's really hard to meet the right kind of guys in a school. What I mean is I'm looking for someone who can have a career where they make enough to live a comfortable life. Teachers don't make enough. There are so few administrators, you know? I thought I needed to work in business for a while. Get my MRS degree. Then I could go back and teach and still have the lifestyle I want."

"I've never heard of an MRS degree, what is that ... Master of Reading Sciences?"

Janie laughs, "You've never heard of an MRS? Practically my whole sorority was working on theirs. About half got them and the rest are still trying."

"Must be a tough degree to get if only half are successful," Genevieve observes, "Guess I'll avoid that one."

Janie smiles, "You've done a pretty good job so far, you have the best part of it in SJ, but without the baggage that generally comes along."

Confused, Genevieve wants to understand, but she realizes it's getting late. She walks Janie to the door, "You know how to get out of here, now?"

Janie nods, gives Genevieve a hug and disappears down the hall.

The next day SJ has a tea party for Ralph and the housekeeping staff. They bring in a back board and set it on the bed, a sheet is the table cloth and chairs and tea cups from the cafeteria for everyone.

Ralph sits on the chair next to SJ. She helps the bear sip his tea.

"This is a very rare oolong tea. That's what Momma drinks," she tells the housekeepers, who also politely sip their tea with their little fingers extended just so, as instructed by SJ.

"Now Mister Ralph doesn't have to extend his little finger because he doesn't have one." SJ laughs at her own joke and the housekeepers do as well.

Dr. Hamilton arrives and asks, "Is this a private party or can any party poopers join?"

SJ turns around and asks, "Have you had your tea today?"

Dr. Hamilton seems to consider her question with as much exaggeration as he can muster and then says with a British accent "By golly I believe I have not had any tea today."

SJ turns back to Mister Ralph, "Well kind sir, please join us. I'm afraid I only have oolong tea. Is that all right?"

"I prefer Earl Gray, because he's a friend of mine, but oolong is acceptable."

SJ pours a cup of water for Dr. Hamilton, as they are only playing it is tea. He takes a sip and raises his nose as high as he can, says, "A jolly good spot there, eh what?"

SJ asks him, "Why are you doing that?"

"What? Putting my nose up in the air? I don't know. I've seen that on television and thought it was what you were supposed to do," he responds.

SJ isn't sure about that so she says, "Let's not do that. Ralph can't bend his neck like that."

"Jolly good then." Dr. Hamilton sips once more and puts the cup back down. "So whose idea was the tea party?"

"Mine." SJ admits, "I asked Tony who usually takes me down for my tests. He took care of everything else. This is so much fun, don't you think?"

"Quite so." Dr. Hamilton responds, then looks at her, evaluating. "So how are you feeling today?"

"I'm all better and ready to go home." The playfulness disappears and the hopefulness lessens as she answers.

"But then who would you have in for tea? Tony wouldn't be able to set it up for you and I would miss you terribly." His response seems strange to SJ. He hesitated before making the last part of his observation.

"You can visit me at Granma's. Then you wouldn't have to miss me and Ralph and I wouldn't have to miss you."

"Who do you think would miss me more, Ralph or you?"

"Well Ralph just met you, and I kinda like your ordeals..."

"Just kind of, huh?" Dr. Hamilton changes the subject, "I'm going away on a short trip here soon and I want to make sure you're all set before I go."

"You're going away?" SJ apparently had not thought he might not

282

be there for her. "Are you going to visit your family?"

"No, I don't have a family, no one to go visit."

"So where are you going?"

"I'm going to Santiago, Chile. Do you know where that is?"

SJ shakes her head.

"It's in South America, an overnight flight from here."

"Why do you want to go there?"

"To figure myself out. Find out what I really want."

"I asked you. Is that why you're going?"

"Maybe. I just need to understand if what I'm doing is enough or whether I want something more."

"You want something more. Tea?" SJ hold up the teapot.

"You're probably right." He holds his cup for her to pour.

The Seventh Ordeal: A Visit to the Underground

That night when Genevieve arrives at the hospital she finds Dr. Hamilton talking with Ralph and SJ.

"But bears can't squeeze into tiny places like that so they have to fish in wide open streams instead." He concludes and when he sees her come in, he stands to greet her.

"Merry un-Bearmas, to you."

"Merry un-Bearmas everyone." She comes over, hugs and kisses for SJ and she provides the same for Ralph.

"No hugs and kisses for Doctor Hamilton?"

Genevieve sees that SJ has been planning this. Genevieve willingly provides the hug and kisses to both cheeks, like the French. He reciprocates.

SJ beams at her small triumph.

"To what do we owe this unanticipated pleasure?" Genevieve asks both the doctor and her scheming daughter.

"Doctor Hamilton thought we should hear about Ralph's last ordeal." SJ tells her.

"I see, and I think it's my turn?" Genevieve realizes.

Dr. Hamilton goes to the intercom and presses the button. No one answers, but the nurses and housekeeping staff all start to wander in and either sit on the window sill or lean against the wall. Tony wheels Jacob in.

Genevieve sits on one side of the bed. Dr. Hamilton sits on the other side with SJ at the head. SJ beams, but then says to them, "This is the end, Momma."

"Okay, kiddo. Let me see. Where did Ralph leave off? So Ralph came back from the Lotus Eaters and the Master of Ordeals gave him the night off. Right?"

SJ nods and shrugs indicating she's close enough.

"So the next day Ralph is summonsed to the massive Hall where the Supreme Bear Council meets. Here the Master of Ordeals waits patiently for Ralph and his parents to arrive. Now Ralph was so happy to have passed his sixth ordeal that he and his parents celebrated with a honey and berry grog. Ralph was a little under the weather the next day."

"You mean he had a hangover?" SJ asks.

Genevieve nods to SJ with a smile and continues, "He is a little late and his father is still in bed. The Master of Ordeals is annoyed. So he spins the Great Ordeal Mixer twice to make sure he gets an especially hard ordeal. Soon, a larger than usual ball drops out.

The Master of Ordeals is grim when he sees this larger ball. He slowly opens it and reads the ordeal to Ralph."

"Why is the ball larger?" SJ wants to know the significance.

"The Master of Ordeals reads the slip of paper, black paper with white ink, saying only, 'Visit the Underground.' Every bear gasps in horror for no bear ever visited the underground and returned to tell the tale."

SJ looks confused.

"Ralph realizes he may never return from this particularly hard ordeal. He looks to his father who has a terrible headache and just arrived. His father holds his head in both paws throughout. Ralph says to his father, 'No bear ever returned from the underground.' And Ralph's father sort of looks at his son and says, 'Your little girl waits for you to prove yourself worthy of her. I believe you are worthy for you are my son. I believe you will visit the underground and come back to us. I have taught you many lessons, but the most important is to believe in yourself and use your imagination to solve problems. I know you will choose to do what is right and what is important. I will wait for your safe return'.

"And Ralph turns to his mother and says, 'Mother, no bear ever returned from the underground." And Ralph's mother hugs her son and says simply, 'Your father and I believe in you.'

"Fearful of the Master of Ordeals, for Ralph knows that he angered him which caused him to draw an impossible ordeal. He asks the Master for directions to the underground. The Master of Ordeals replies 'There are many ways to the underground. Most involve making bad decisions, but others involve making noble choices. You must decide how you will arrive in this place.'

"It becomes abundantly clear to Ralph why no bear ever returned. Then he looks at the Master of Ordeals and asks, 'How will I know when I have successfully overcome this Ordeal?'

"The Master of Ordeals replies, 'If you demonstrate the ability to transcend this life you will be deemed successful.'

"Ralph's father listens and is so fearful for his son that he tells the Master of Ordeals, 'Transcendence is impossible.'

"The Master of Ordeals shows anger that a father would question his selection. He replies, 'I will say no more.'"

"Sounds like you're in deep doo doo, Ralph." SJ shakes her head.

"So Ralph, who is even more affectionate, thinking to himself that he will probably never return from the underground, goes to his father and gives him tearful hugs and kisses. Then to his mother who refuses to kiss him goodbye. Ralph says to his mother, 'Why will you not kiss and hug me goodbye?' And she says to her only son, 'I will not say good bye, only so long, expecting you will come back to me.'

"Ralph cannot believe his mother will not say goodbye to him. Heartbroken, he leaves the Great Hall. Ralph stops people on the street and asks 'do you know the way to the underground?' Most people simply shake their head as they walk by. One older white haired woman stops and has to think a moment. 'Yes, dear. My husband and I visited London last year. We went everywhere by the underground. They have a sign that says Mind the Gap. I think it was a red circle with a line through it.'

Ralph walks down street after street looking for the red circle sign with a line through it. He stops and asks people: 'Where do I mind the gap?' But people again shake their heads and keep walking.

"It seems to Ralph that he will never find a way to reach the underground. He sees a man wearing a uniform coming his way. The uniform is green and he has what look like medals on his chest.

"'Could you help me find the underground? I need to endure one more ordeal and then I'll have a Bearmas and a little girl of my very own.' Ralph asks the man who he sees has stripes on his shoulders.

"'Mister Bear my friends and I endure more ordeals than you can imagine. We help protect every little boy and girl in our country. Often in others as well. We would be proud if you joined us. If you're unlucky, you might end up in the underground. But that's not what we hope for any of our recruits.'

"This is the first person who has said he would endure ordeals and might get to the underground. So Ralph follows the man in the uniform back to his office.

"Ralph enlisted on the spot, after only one more honey and berry grog, this time courtesy of the recruiter. He goes through basic training where he loses twenty-five pounds and learns to shoot a gun. His platoon is sent overseas almost immediately to a war zone where his team patrols a rural village. On his first day in the village his team patrols along a flooded fast running river. They hear a scream, a splash and a call for help. He has lost so much weight and is in such good shape that Ralph is the first one to react to the sound. In the rapids a little girl, not more than five years old is carried along bobbing under and back to the surface. Her mother calls to her baby from the bridge. It is clear that the girl fell from the bridge. Ralph doesn't hesitate a second. He dives into the water and swims as fast as he can against a fast running current. He reaches the little girl and brings her to a large boulder in the middle of the stream. He has worked so hard to reach her that he is too tired to swim back carrying her. So he calls for his team. They come out on the bridge and build a rope chair for the little girl. They throw it to Ralph. But the stream is so strong they can't get the rope chair to him. So Ralph has them throw it one more time. He swims with the little girl on his back, using all of his strength to reach where the rope chair hangs under the bridge. Even though he is very tired, he helps her into the rope chair and signals his team mates pull her back up. But because she is downstream from the bridge, she would be dragged through the water if they just pull on the rope. So Ralph swims with the rope chair and the little girl in it on his shoulders until they are directly under the bridge. His team is able to pull the little girl to safety and reunite her with her mother. But Ralph is exhausted. He can't fight against the current any longer. The fast moving waters carry him away. Ralph tries to make it to shore, but he is slammed against large rocks in the stream, one after another. He is dunked under and barely has strength to fight back to the surface. Finally he smashes head on into a large boulder and he passes out … and he drowns."

"He drowns?" SJ cannot believe it. "My poor Ralph."

288

"Ralph wakes up in the underground where he meets Peter the Great. The Great Black Bear that is Peter the Great says to Ralph, 'Why did you save the little girl at the expense of your own life?' And Ralph replies, 'I came to the underground to prove myself worthy of a little girl who waits for me. But if I did not save that little girl in the river, I would not be a worthy bear. So, you see, I had no choice. Even if that meant I might never have a little girl of my own.

"Peter the Great had never met a bear as humble as Ralph. He decided to write a letter to the Master of the Ordeals saying that Ralph visited the underground. He is the first bear that ever demonstrated transcendence. His actions are so worthy that for the first time a bear that reached the underground is being returned to the world above. Therefore, he recommended that Ralph be recognized as completing the ordeal, and be deemed worthy.

"The next thing Ralph knows he is back home. His mother and father hug and kiss him for he has been to the underground and returned to them. He hands the letter from Peter the Great to the Master of the Ordeals. The Master reads the letter to the Supreme Bear Council. They say Hallelujah, for Ralph has demonstrated not only the transcendent virtues of a true bear, but also his worthiness by sacrificing himself for a little girl. And since he is the only bear ever to have returned from the underground, he is declared worthy. A Bearmas is authorized and his ticket to meet SJ, his new little girl is handed him by the Master of the Ordeals."

Exhausted from telling the Ordeal, Genevieve looks around. Everyone in the room dries a tear, including Dr. Hamilton. Then the nurses both begin to clap together. The housekeepers join in. SJ gives her mother the biggest hug ever.

Overcome by the reaction to the ordeal, Genevieve notices that one of the nurses has a small tape recorder going, which she now clicks off.

Dr. Hamilton, gives her a hug.

"It should be a bear hug." SJ calls out to them. Dr. Hamilton gives Genevieve that bear hug. She hugs him back, thinking it would be nice to have bear hugs more often, like at least once a day.

The housekeepers and the nurses file out. Each one comes to Genevieve and tells her how much they loved the ordeal. They thought it was better than Dr. Hamilton's ordeal, but they would appreciate it if she didn't tell him that. Of course Dr. Hamilton over hears and just shrugs to them and winks.

The orderly comes for Jacob who has fallen asleep in his wheelchair. As Jacob is wheeled out, Genevieve says to Dr. Hamilton, "Jacob doesn't look good."

Dr. Hamilton watches Jacob leave but doesn't respond. He then turns and sits down next to SJ and Ralph.

SJ looks puzzled, "He's so big. Why is he so big if he's not a redeemed bear?"

Dr. Hamilton doesn't miss a beat, "It's because he has such a big heart it would never fit in a smaller bear."

SJ nods in understanding, but then asks, "So he knows how to catch salmon and make baklava even though he was never a redeeming bear?"

Genevieve nods, "Of course, SJ. Papa bears teach all their children how to fish for salmon and Momma bears teach all their children how to make baklava."

Dr. Hamilton smiles at her, "Good answer."

"But I don't have a Poppa bear. Does that mean I'll never learn to fish for salmon?" SJ realizes.

"I'll teach you to fish for salmon, as soon as you're well." Dr. Hamilton offers.

"I'm well now. Will you take me tomorrow?"

"Not tomorrow, but soon."

"In Chile? Do they have salmon, in Chile?" SJ watches Dr. Hamilton.

"Sure, if that's where you want to learn to fish, then Chile it is." Dr. Hamilton winks at SJ. Genevieve looks at both of them with a puzzled expression.

The Final Test

The next morning Genevieve finishes brushing out her hair looking in the hospital bathroom mirror. SJ is not yet awake, but some mornings she is up early and some not. Genevieve goes over to her daughter, kisses her now completely bald head, but still the child does not wake up. Genevieve smiles at the sentinel Ralph, guarding her baby from the cancer that maliciously tries to take her away. She picks up the bear, gives him a hug and a kiss on the top of his head.

On her way out she stops by the nurse's station and tells the nurse that SJ is sleeping in today so she didn't disturb her. The nurse mentions how much she liked the ordeal and how she tied it all together, but how sad she was that there wouldn't be any more ordeals to listen to.

A half hour later Genevieve walks into her cubicle, checks the messages and gets started on her intakes. Another busy day awaits, but she notices that one of the messages is from her mother. She decides to wait and call her when she would be up. She started sleeping in after SJ went to the hospital, since she didn't have to be up early when Genevieve dropped SJ off.

About ten o'clock her mother calls her.

"Hi, Mom. How's things?"

"Great. I've met someone. He's everything you father was not."

Dead silence continues at both ends of the line for too long. Then Genevieve replies, "I'm happy for you."

"Well I don't want to count my chickens and all that, but if this works out I plan to sell this old house and move in with him."

Again Genevieve doesn't respond. She knows what her mother is saying. Sell the house. Move in with him. All of which leaves Genevieve without a home … once again.

"Tell me about him." Genevieve finally decides to ask.

"I've actually known him forever. He's the older brother of a friend. Fantastic dancer, gourmet cook, loves to travel and absolutely fabulous in bed. I can't begin to tell you…"

"Don't bother, mother. How long before you make a decision about moving?" Genevieve doesn't know what else to say.

"We're going to Toronto for a romantic weekend. I think he's going to pop the question then. Of course I'll say yes and move immediately when we get back."

"So, soon."

"I don't mean to put you out dear…"

"Well you are… literally. Goodbye, Mother." Genevieve hangs up and it feels like the whole world has dropped through a never ending series of trap doors. Just when she thinks there's something to hold onto another trap door opens.

She opens the bottom drawer to her desk, takes out the GED study guide and tosses it into the trash can. *Damn it what's the use? I owe my soul to the company store.* But then she gets angry. She reaches over and extracts the guide and puts it back in the drawer. Places the apple back on top. *I'm ready for the test. It's a pay increase, which I need even more now. One step at a time. One day at a time. Tomorrow is another day. One more day with SJ. You can do this.*

At one-thirty Genevieve goes to the courtyard and studies for her test, scheduled for the next day, Saturday. She thinks she knows everything necessary to pass, but wants to review the math section tonight before going to bed. Hopefully the formulas will be fresh in her mind.

When her hour is up, she tries to answer one more question. The door to the courtyard comes swinging open and Janie comes running though. Genevieve looks up, puzzled by her expression.

"You need to call Doctor Hamilton as soon as possible. He said it's not an emergency, but he wants to talk to you before you return to the hospital." Janie explains.

Genevieve pushes past Janie to get back to her desk. She has the number memorized, although she has only called it a few times. The long ring and then the receptionist.

"Heinz, Hamilton and Walker, can I help you?"

"MaryAlice, this is Genevieve Wilcox. Doctor Hamilton left a message for me to call as soon as possible."

"Yes, Miss Wilcox. Let me locate him for you." The muzak only serves to fuel her anxiety, not soothe her tension. She soon finds herself counting the number of songs she listens to, reminding her how long she waits. She thinks they should use long version songs, just so the whole process isn't so annoying.

Then he is there, "Genevieve. It's Jackson. I've got some bad news. I wanted you to have some time to adjust. Before you get here tonight."

Oh God, what more can happen? She was great yesterday. Please let it be minor.

"Okay, what is it?"

294

"Remember we talked about the possible alternatives?"

"Yes, the rosy scenario and the worst case analysis, obviously the rosy scenario is off the table."

"I'm afraid so." Dr. Hamilton sounds truly sad. It drives her into a corner of her mind where she just goes through the motions. The words no longer causing an emotional reaction.

"Surgery?" She hears her voice say, but she doesn't remember thinking or saying anything to him.

"The tumor has stopped shrinking. In order for her to be cancer free, I'm afraid Doctor Grant needs to do the surgery. He needs to do it today."

"Today?" Genevieve tries to understand the need to act so quickly. "Why today."

"If it's not shrinking anymore, it will may start growing again. We need to get it out when it's as small as it's going to get. In my judgment, that's now."

"I trust your judgment."

That night Genevieve attempts to sleep on the chair in SJ's room. The bandages cover most of SJ's head like a turban. Ralph sits above her, guarding like the silent sentinel he has become. Dr. Grant told her after the surgery all had gone as expected, but they wouldn't know if they got everything until the pathology report came back from the lab. That would be a day or two. SJ had been awake when they brought her back from recovery, but she soon fell asleep. Genevieve tried to get some sleep while she had the chance.

"Granma ... here? SJ asks.

"No. She went on a trip with a friend, but she'll be back to see you soon."

That was the only question. Apparently she went back to sleep. So Genevieve did the same.

Saturday morning. Genevieve reads Great Expectations to SJ. A long book, she chose it off the shelf at her mother's house knowing it will take them a while to get through. She thought the title was appropriate even if the story was going to be hard for SJ to understand. But much of their conversations tended around explanations Genevieve had to give SJ so she could understand some level of the story they were reading. Since there would be no more ordeals for Ralph, she needed something that would keep SJ's attention for a long time.

Genevieve hears a knock at the door. She looks up and finds Janie and Dean carrying two thermos bottles and a dozen crispy crèmes.

"What are you doing?" Genevieve asks.

Janie pipes up, "You have a test to take in a half hour. We're your relief. Coffee since we knew you wouldn't sleep and sugar to get you through it. Now get your bag, your pencils and get going."

"I can't possibly…"

"You told me she most wanted you to make something more out of yourself than you are. She wants you to do this." Dean set the coffee and donuts on the shelf. "We're not taking no for an answer."

"I can't leave her now."

"She wants you to do this. We'll pick up where you left off. Now since we're drinking coffee here you better hurry or we'll have a problem.

Too tired to fight Genevieve picks up her things. She heads off for the test with coffee and crispy crèmes under her arm.

Five hours later Genevieve walks back into the familiar hospital room. She hears the sound of Dean reading Great Expectations. Janie chats with Ralph. When she comes into the room, SJ remains sitting, alert and listening to both the story, but also the conversation that Janie has with Ralph.

Genevieve goes to SJ, gives her daughter a hug, "Hi, hon. I took the test, it wasn't easy but I got through it. I wouldn't have been able to do that without your help studying."

SJ kisses her mother's hair.

Janie looks at her, "Why don't you get a couple hours sleep. We can stay."

"You've done so much already, I can't ask…" she starts to protest, but Janie will have none of it and shoos her off to get some sleep.

Four hours later she groggily re-enters the hospital room. Janie now reads from Great Expectations. Dean drinks the last of the coffee. SJ remains sitting up but her eyes are closed. She seems to be breathing easily.

"Hi. Guess I was more tired than I realized. Look I really appreciate you doing this for me."

"We wanted to and besides this is fun." Janie looks tired, but remains bubbly.

Dean comes by and gives her a hug, "I'm proud of you. Just hang in there. I'll stop by tomorrow to give you another spell."

"We'll stop by. I wouldn't miss another play day." Janie adds.

"I can't thank you enough." Genevieve walks them to the door. She checks on SJ again.

"I'm back, baby. Everything all right?"

SJ doesn't respond, but her breathing remains regular.

Genevieve settles down in the chair and takes up reading aloud from Great Expectations where Janie left off.

On Monday morning the sun peeks through the windows of the hospital room. Genevieve sleeps sitting up in the chair, Great Expectations closed on her lap. She wears the same clothes as Saturday when she took her test. SJ stirs and puts her hand on Ralph, snuggles with him. She also appears to sleep with a bit of frown.

The door opens admitting Granma, who carries an overnight bag. Her hair askew and her clothes wrinkled. She seems at loose ends. Genevieve begins to stir, wakened by the sound of the door opening.

"How's she ... my god, what did they do to her?" Genevieve's mother exclaims not knowing about the surgery.

Genevieve stretches as she tries to wake up, responds through a yawn, "Dr. Grant removed the tumor on Friday."

"And you didn't call me? I would have come straight back."

"You didn't leave until Friday. From my last conversation with you, I thought your priorities were pretty clear. So you a married lady yet?"

Her mother stiffens, "If you're trying to make me…"

"I'm not trying to do anything other than pay bills, mother." Genevieve already dreads having to move out of her childhood home. She looks at SJ, with Ralph watching over her. She thinks of the ordeals they have shared; only SJ's ordeal has been real and Ralph's set of fanciful stories.

She rises, puts the book down and picks up the juice glass with a straw that rests next to SJ. As she looks up, she notices her mother seems to be waiting for something.

"Well … aren't you even going to ask?" Her mother watches Genevieve clear the table beside SJ's bed. "Don't you care?"

"Frankly mother, I could ask you the very same question."

Her mother glances over her shoulder, "Just the fact that you're here must mean she's getting better."

Genevieve just looks at her mother, unable to form words in response.

With no response, Granma looks puzzled. She glances back at SJ, trying to put two and two together.

"Well you don't have to worry about moving for now, if that's the bee in your bonnet."

"Mother … that's just the most recent way you've failed us over the years."

"I still don't know why you dislike me so much. I raised you and sent you on your way. When you got into trouble I could have just said go figure it out, but no, I passed on a promotion and worked from home for the last seven years so you could go to work. What thanks do I get for that? Just this icy coldness and blame from you. As if I was the one who got you pregnant at sixteen. As if I were the one who decided to keep the child, when everyone told you to give her up for adoption. As if I were the one who made you refuse to finish school so you could get a job, when that asshole who got you pregnant denied it was his kid. You could have insisted on a blood test you know. But no … you said you'd rather not have him part of your life if that was the way he was going to be. And now that she's sick it's my fault again. As if I passed on genes that caused her cancer or something. I'm just trying to get on with my own life here. Can't you understand that? I've given you everything you should have needed. I didn't sign up to give up my life for you. I want to be loved again. I want someone to think I'm pretty! Someone who wants to be with me, because I'm desirable. I'm a good person, but I just want to have a life of my own, can't you see that?"

Genevieve glances at her mother without responding and looks at her daughter for a long moment. SJ's eyes open and flutter. Then she focuses in and sees her mother. A big smile. "It doesn't hurt anymore, Mama. My head doesn't hurt." SJ turns her head and sees her grandmother. "Granma. My head doesn't hurt anymore."

The End of the Ordeals

Genevieve finds Dr. Hamilton waiting for them when SJ is finally discharged from the hospital.

"How are you getting home?" he asks.

"I had to sell my car to pay bills so we're taking the bus."

Dr. Hamilton consults his watch. "If you can wait about thirty minutes I can give you a ride home. I'm leaving early today to pack for a trip."

"Your Chile trip?" Genevieve asks.

The doctor nods and then disappears. Genevieve entertains SJ in the lobby as they wait. Dr. Hamilton doesn't take the whole half hour. He returns without his lab coat, which he has replaced with a brown jacket and a smile.

Genevieve looks at his new Mercedes and thinks to herself that she will never own a car like his. She hopes SJ appreciates this special treat.

As they exit the hospital garage, Dr. Hamilton observes, "You seem preoccupied. What are you worried about?"

"Everything. My mother has a new job and can't care for SJ anymore. I've used up all my time at work. If I go out on Family Medical Leave I'll won't be paid. And I've got to get started on college classes or I'll never make enough to pay all the bills I have."

Dr. Hamilton glances at her, but keeps his eyes on the road. "I've arranged for SJ to use our day treatment center until she can go back to

301

school. Then she'll be able to come after school. We even have a bus that will pick her up and bring her to the hospital if you can pick her up after work."

"My insurance won't pay for it." Genevieve is hard at work trying to fit everything into what she knows she can afford.

"You won't have to pay. That's covered."

"How? Who?" Genevieve tries to put it all together.

"While I'm away I'd like you to think about something." His question interrupts her thoughts.

"You're going to Chile?" SJ asks. "You still have to teach me to fish."

Genevieve remembers thinking that people like doctors go to Chile, but an insurance claims assistant can only dream of such places.

"Yes, SJ, I'm going to Chile. I'm going to try to figure some things out. You know, I've never known what it is I want out of life. I'm hoping when I return I'll know." Genevieve listens to the confusion in his voice, the pain and fear of discovering things he really doesn't want to know.

"What do you want me to think about?" She is almost afraid to ask, but thinks she might know.

"What you want out of life now that you have a chance to start over. You're a very special person." He checks her expression just before turning into the driveway at that old familiar house she expects won't be home much longer.

"We talked before about how people like you go to Chile and people like me have to claw through life just to survive."

"Don't put limits on yourself that may not really be there. Open your mind to the possible." He turns off the engine.

302

"And what should I do, once I've decided?" She asks of this man who gave so much to ensure SJ's recovery.

"Call me."

Dr. Hamilton leans over and kisses her for a long magic moment. This is the kiss she so wanted. But what does it mean?

And when the magic moment passes, she and SJ get out of the car. They wait as he backs into the familiar old street. The cold wind causes her to shiver. Genevieve checks SJ to make sure she's warm enough. She checks the fast moving clouds above that threaten rain, then returns her gaze to Dr. Hamilton.

From the front window of the old house, built by a doctor more than a century before, Ralph the Bear watches his very own little girl, who, now that Ralph has arrived, is getting stronger every day. He also looks after his special friend the doctor. This is the same doctor who gave him his name. Ralph wishes the doctor would find a way to bring Sadie to live with him. Maybe Jacob could come for a tea party too. Ralph wonders how bear wishes become reality like his wish that SJ gets better has. And as Ralph watches, the doctor exchanges a lingering look with Genevieve, and slowly drives away. SJ and her mother wave good-bye.

About the Author

dhtreichler toured the global garden spots as a defense contractor executive for fifteen years. His assignments covered intelligence, training and battlefield systems integrating state of the art technology to keep Americans safe. During this time he authored seven novels exploring the role of increasingly sophisticated technology in transforming our lives and how men and women establish relationships in a mediated world.

Keep up with all of dhtreichler's latest work and essays at www.dhtreichler.com.

Also by dhtreichler

The Ghost in the Machine: a novel

Life After

The Tragic Flaw

Succession

The End Game

I Believe in You

Rik's

The Illustrated Bearmas Reader – Ralph's Ordeals

The First Bearmas

Made in the USA
Lexington, KY
04 July 2018